World Economics Association

Book Series

Volume 3

GW00985275

Developing an economics for the
post-crisis world

Titles produced by the World Economics Association & College Publications

Piketty's *Capital in the Twenty-First Century*
Edward Fullbrook and Jamie Morgan, eds.

Volume 1
The Economics Curriculum: Towards a Radical reformulation
Maria Alejandra Maki and Jack Reardon, eds.

Volume 2
Finance as Warfare
Michael Hudson

Volume 3
Developing an economics for the post-crisis world
Steve Keen

Volume 4
On the use and misuse of theories and models in mainstream economics
Lars Pålsson Syll

The **World Economics Association (WEA)** was launched on May 16, 2011. Already over 13,000 economists and related scholars have joined. This phenomenal success has come about because the WEA fills a huge gap in the international community of economists – the absence of a professional organization which is truly international and pluralist.

The World Economics Association seeks to increase the relevance, breadth and depth of economic thought. Its key qualities are worldwide membership and governance, and inclusiveness with respect to: (a) the variety of theoretical perspectives; (b) the range of human activities and issues which fall within the broad domain of economics; and (c) the study of the world's diverse economies.

The Association's activities centre on the development, promotion and diffusion of economic research and knowledge and on illuminating their social character.

The WEA publishes 20+ books a year, three open-access journals *(Economic Thought, World Economic Review* and *Real-World Economics Review)*, a bi-monthly newsletter, blogs, holds global online conferences, runs a textbook commentaries project and an eBook library.

www.worldeconomicassociation.org

Developing an economics for the post-crisis world

Steve Keen

ISBN 978-1-84890-186-5 print
ISBN 978-1-911156-09-3 eBook-PDF

Published by College Publications on behalf of the World Economics
Association
College Publications
Scientific Director: Dov Gabbay
Managing Director: Jane Spurr

http://www.worldeconomicsassociation.org
http://www.collegepublications.co.uk

Front cover image – detail from *Temple Gardens* (1920) by Paul Klee

Cover design by Laraine Welch
Printed by Lightning Source, Milton Keynes, UK

Contents

Developing an economics for the post-crisis world

Introduction

The veracity of mainstream economics has been called into question in the years since the economic crisis began. But the questioning of economics precedes the crisis, and not by merely years but arguably ever since 1898, when Thorstein Veblen published his brilliant paper "Why is Economics not an Evolutionary Science?" But Veblen's critique fell on the deaf ears of the mainstream, and was unknown to the public. Only in the fringes of academic economists did Veblen's words, and the spirit of rebellion he encouraged, live on.

Economics came under challenge again in the 1930s, and this time Keynes led the charge against an orthodoxy that, six years after the Great Depression began, had no idea what caused it, or how to overcome it. But Keynes's challenge was largely deflected by Hicks's reinterpretation of Keynes, and the taxonomic economics that Veblen hoped to defeat was rebuilt after the challenge of the Great Depression and the World War had ended.

In 2007, the global economy experienced its greatest crisis since the Great Depression, and once again, mainstream economics failed to anticipate the crisis, and even after it has apparently passed – in the Anglo-Saxon world at least – once again, can provide no explanation of why it happened in the first place.

What is different this time around is that there is a publicly accessible outlet for critical voices, and it has been around – in various guises – for 15 years. What was first known as PAECON (the Protest against Autistic ECONomics) and is now known as the Real World Economics Review was established by Edward Fullbrook in 2000 in response to protests by French students against the unworldly theorems they were forced to learn in the French economics curriculum. When the financial crisis hit in late 2007, the Real World Economics Review was already there, ready to provide an outlet for critical economists, and intent on getting their views to the public.

Developing an economics for the post-crisis world

This short book provides the articles that I have published in RWER over the last fifteen years – starting with the first in July 2001. The topics covered include methodology, microeconomics, and the monetary approach to macroeconomics that I have been developing – along with many other non-mainstream economists – over the last 20 years.

As economics itself should do, my views have evolved over this time – and especially my macroeconomics. I began with the development of a mathematical model Minsky's Financial Instability Hypothesis (Keen 1995). That model simulated a debt-crisis, but it involved treating the monetary side of capitalism implicitly – by linking the change in private debt to the level of investment, but without including an explicit banking sector in the model. Yet it was obvious from the outset that the phenomenon that Basil Moore described as endogenous money (Moore 1979) had to play a vital role in macroeconomics. To make that possible, a method for building strictly monetary models of capitalism had to be constructed (which led to the development of the Open Source system dynamics program Minsky – see http://sourceforge.net/projects/minsky/), and the logic of how endogenous money altered macroeconomics had to be developed.

My explanation began from the intuition that the change in debt was an integral part of aggregate demand. My initial expression of it – which is reproduced in this book – was that aggregate demand was "income plus the change in debt". However to many other non-mainstream economists, this had to be a fallacy, since it implied that expenditure and income were not identical, when they have to be (Fiebiger 2014, Lavoie 2014).

The critics were right – but so was my intuition. Just recently I have, I believe, reconciled the two, to show that aggregate demand and aggregate income are equal to expenditure and income financed out of existing money, plus expenditure and income generated by the change in debt. The full argument will be published later this year (Keen 2015, Keen 2015), but since it is so central to the continuing relevance of several chapters in this book, I feel that I have to go beyond the typical confines of an introduction and provide the essence of the argument here.

Introduction

My first attempts to explain how the change in debt could have a role in both expenditure and income relied upon seeing a new debt as a discontinuous injection into a continuous flow of expenditure and income, which were identical except at the point of the injection – see Figure 1 – though measurement over that discontinuity (which is essentially integration, or working out the area beneath the functions across a time period) would show them as being identical.

Figure 1 Portraying the role of change in debt in expenditure and income as a discontinuity (Figure 2 in Keen 2014, p. 285)

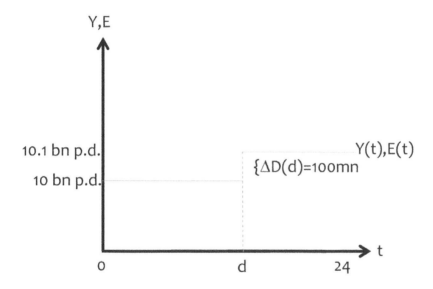

However critics could not accept this, since it implied a difference in what are identities in economics: expenditure *is* income. As Fiebiger put it:

> Unless Keen (2014a) can explain how a purchase of a good or service does not provide income for the seller, then he should rethink his claim that debt extensions can force an inequality between expenditure and income at the aggregate level (Fiebiger 2014, p. 296).

This criticism inspired the thought that, if the intuition that change in debt was a factor in aggregate demand was correct, then it should be possible to derive it from an expenditure table. Consider a 3 sector economy in which expenditure by one sector becomes income for the other two. Label expenditure out of existing money as E_{xy}, where x is the spending sector and y is the receiving sector – thus expenditure by sector 2 buying the outputs of sector 3 is E_{23}.

In a world where borrowing and lending are not possible – so all expenditure has to be financed out of existing money – that results in the pattern shown in Table 1. Aggregate expenditure is the negative sum of the diagonal of the table; aggregate income is the sum of the off-diagonal elements. They are necessarily equal.

Table 1: No borrowing or lending is possible (Case A)

Activity\Sector	Sector 1	Sector 2	Sector 3
Sector 1 Expenditure	$-(E_{1,2} + E_{1,3})$	$E_{1,2}$	$E_{1,3}$
Sector 2 Expenditure	$E_{2,1}$	$-(E_{2,1} + E_{2,3})$	$E_{2,3}$
Sector 3 Expenditure	$E_{3,1}$	$E_{3,2}$	$-(E_{3,1} + E_{3,2})$

Equation (1.1) shows aggregate demand AD_A and aggregate income AY_A for case (A).

$$AD_A = \left(E_{1,2} + E_{1,3}\right) + \left(E_{2,1} + E_{2,3}\right) + \left(E_{3,1} + E_{3,2}\right)$$
$$AY_A = E_{1,2} + E_{1,3} + E_{2,1} + E_{2,3} + E_{3,1} + E_{3,2}$$

(1.1)

Now consider the empirically false "Loanable Funds" model of lending followed by Neoclassical economists, in which lending is a transfer from one sector (or agent in Neoclassical parlance) to another. Sector 2 reduces its spending by ΔD to make a loan of ΔD to sector 1, which then immediately spends it buying the output of sectors 2 and 3; Sector 1 spends the borrowed money in the proportions α and $(1-\alpha)$ on the outputs of sectors 2 and 3, while sector 2's reduction in expenditure is distributed in the proportions β and *(1- β)* over sectors 1 and 3. This results in the situation shown in Table 2.

Table 2: Borrowing and lending between sectors occurs (Case B: Loanable Funds)

Activity\Sector	Sector 1	Sector 2	Sector 3
Sector 1 Expenditure	$-([E_{1,2} + \alpha.\Delta D] + [E_{1,3} + (1-\alpha).\Delta D])$	$E_{1,2} + \alpha.\Delta D$	$E_{1,3} + (1-\alpha).\Delta D$
Sector 2 Expenditure	$E_{2,1} - \beta.\Delta D$	$-([E_{2,1} - \beta.\Delta D] + [E_{2,3} - (1-\beta).\Delta D])$	$E_{2,3} - (1-\beta).\Delta D]$
Sector 3 Expenditure	$E_{3,1}$	$E_{3,2}$	$-(E_{3,1} + E_{3,2})$

When aggregate expenditure and aggregate income are summed, the same result applies as for the case with no lending:

$$AD_B = \left(E_{1,2}+E_{1,3}\right)+\left(E_{2,1}+E_{2,3}\right)+\left(E_{3,1}+E_{3,2}\right)$$
$$AY_B = E_{1,2}+E_{1,3}+E_{2,1}+E_{2,3}+E_{3,1}+E_{3,2}$$

$$(1.2)$$

Now consider the real-world situation of a bank lending ΔD to sector 1. This loan increases sector 1's spending without causing an off-setting reduction in spending by any other sector, as shown in Table 3.

Developing an economics for the post-crisis world

Table 3: Borrowing from and lending by banks occurs (Case C: Endogenous Money)

Activity\ Sector	Sector 1	Sector 2	Sector 3
Sector 1 Expenditure	$-([E_{1,2}+ \alpha.\Delta D] + [E_{1,3} + (1-\alpha).\Delta D])$	$E_{1,2}+ \alpha.\Delta D$	$E_{1,3} + (1-\alpha).\Delta D$
Sector 2 Expenditure	$E_{2,1}$	$-(E_{2,1} + E_{2,3})$	$E_{2,3}$
Sector 3 Expenditure	$E_{3,1}$	$E_{3,2}$	$-(E_{3,1} + E_{3,2})$

Summing aggregate expenditure and aggregate income yields the expressions shown in equation (1.3):

$$AD_C = \Delta D + \left(E_{1,2} + E_{1,3}\right) + \left(E_{2,1} + E_{2,3}\right) + \left(E_{3,1} + E_{3,2}\right)$$
$$AY_C = \Delta D + \left(E_{1,2} + E_{1,3}\right) + \left(E_{2,1} + E_{2,3}\right) + \left(E_{3,1} + E_{3,2}\right)$$

(1.3)

The change in debt turns up as an argument in *both* aggregate demand and aggregate income. The only way to sensibly interpret this is that *aggregate demand equals demand generated out of the turnover of existing money, plus demand generated by the creation of new money through the change in debt, and this causes an equivalent change in aggregate income.*

The previous expositions considered an instantaneous injection of new debt, and ignored the motive for lending – the payment of interest to the lender. However the same general conclusions apply when we consider a continuous flow of new debt, and interest payments on existing debt and deposit accounts. In Figure 2, S_1, S_2 and S_3 represent the deposit accounts of each sector, flows are specified using time constants so that τ_{xy} represents the rate at which sector x's account balance is spent buying the outputs of sector y, B_E represents the equity of the banking sector, through which interest payments are made, and r_D and r_L represent the rate of interest on deposits and loans respectively:

Figure 2: Table of monetary flows with continuous flow of new debt

	S_1	S_2	S_3	B_E
Exp_{S1}	$-\left(\dfrac{S_1}{\tau_{12}} + \dfrac{S_1}{\tau_{13}} + \dfrac{d}{dt}D + r_L \cdot D\right)$	$\dfrac{S_1}{\tau_{12}} + \alpha \cdot \dfrac{d}{dt}D$	$\dfrac{S_1}{\tau_{13}} + (1-\alpha) \cdot \dfrac{d}{dt}D$	$r_L \cdot D$
Exp_{S2}	$\dfrac{S_2}{\tau_{21}}$	$-\left(\dfrac{S_2}{\tau_{21}} + \dfrac{S_2}{\tau_{23}}\right)$	$\dfrac{S_2}{\tau_{23}}$	0
Exp_{S3}	$\dfrac{S_3}{\tau_{31}}$	$\dfrac{S_3}{\tau_{32}}$	$-\left(\dfrac{S_3}{\tau_{31}} + \dfrac{S_3}{\tau_{32}}\right)$	0
Exp_B	$\dfrac{B_E}{\tau_{B1}} + r_D \cdot S_1$	$\dfrac{B_E}{\tau_{B2}} + r_D \cdot S_2$	$\dfrac{B_E}{\tau_{B3}} + r_D \cdot S_3$	$-\left(\dfrac{B_E}{\tau_{B1}} + \dfrac{B_E}{\tau_{B2}} + \dfrac{B_E}{\tau_{B3}}\right) - r_D \cdot (S_1 + S_2 + S_3)$

The aggregate expenditure and aggregate income expressions for this situation are shown in Equation (1.4).

$$AD_{EM} = \left(\frac{1}{\tau_{1,2}} + \frac{1}{\tau_{1,3}}\right) \cdot S_1 + \left(\frac{1}{\tau_{2,1}} + \frac{1}{\tau_{2,3}}\right) \cdot S_2 + \left(\frac{1}{\tau_{3,1}} + \frac{1}{\tau_{3,2}}\right) \cdot S_3$$

$$+ \left(\frac{1}{\tau_{B,1}} + \frac{1}{\tau_{B,2}} + \frac{1}{\tau_{B,3}}\right) \cdot B_E + r_D \cdot \left(S_1 + S_2 + S_3\right) + r_L \cdot D + \frac{d}{dt}D$$

(1.4)

$$AY_{EM} = \left(\frac{1}{\tau_{1,2}} + \frac{1}{\tau_{1,3}}\right) \cdot S_1 + \left(\frac{1}{\tau_{2,1}} + \frac{1}{\tau_{2,3}}\right) \cdot S_2 + \left(\frac{1}{\tau_{3,1}} + \frac{1}{\tau_{3,2}}\right) \cdot S_3$$

$$+ \left(\frac{1}{\tau_{B,1}} + \frac{1}{\tau_{B,2}} + \frac{1}{\tau_{B,3}}\right) \cdot B_E + r_D \cdot \left(S_1 + S_2 + S_3\right) + r_L \cdot D + \frac{d}{dt}D$$

Aggregate demand and aggregate income therefore include:

- Expenditure financed by existing money (the first 4 terms); plus
- Gross financial transactions – both interest on debt and interest on deposits (the next two terms); plus
- The change in debt.

This logical argument thus explains the correlations that articles reproduced in this volume found between change in debt and the level of unemployment and asset prices, and between acceleration in debt and change in both unemployment and asset prices. Since the latest paper in this volume was published in 2013, I have updated the key graphs here.

US debt levels

These graphs indicate that, while the crisis that began in late 2007 in the USA is over, the cause of that crisis – a debt bubble on an already excessive level of private debt – has not been eliminated as it was after the Great Depression and the Second World War.

Introduction

Firstly, using comparable data – generated by combining Federal Reserve debt data from 1945 till now with Census debt data from 1916 till 1970 and Census bank loan data from 1834 till 1970 – the ratio of private debt to GDP reached its highest level ever during this crisis, while the amount of deleveraging that occurred was relatively trivial. This implies that the current recovery will be short-lived, since the headroom available for growth in debt levels is minimal.

Figure 3: Aggregate US private debt to GDP

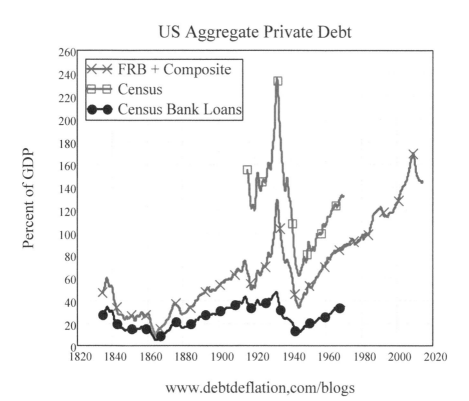

www.debtdeflation.com/blogs

Secondly, the causal relationships between change in debt and the level of unemployment, and between the acceleration of debt and change in unemployment, are robust. The strength of the correlations imply that economic data today are dominated by both the scale and the volatility of change in debt.

Figure 4: Change in debt drives the level of economic activity

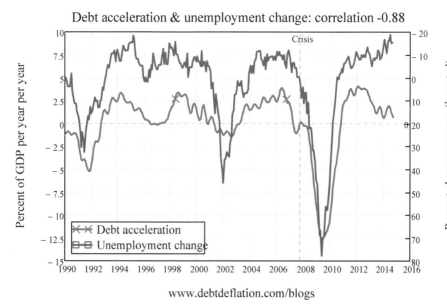

US Private debt change & unemployment: correlation -0.93

www.debtdeflation.com/blogs

Figure 5: Acceleration in debt drives the change in economic activity

Debt acceleration & unemployment change: correlation -0.88

www.debtdeflation.com/blogs

Figure 6: Mortgage acceleration drives house price change

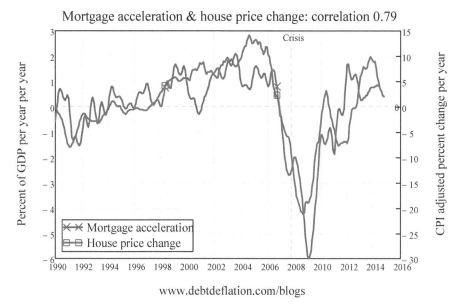

www.debtdeflation.com/blogs

Figure 7: Margin debt acceleration drives share price change

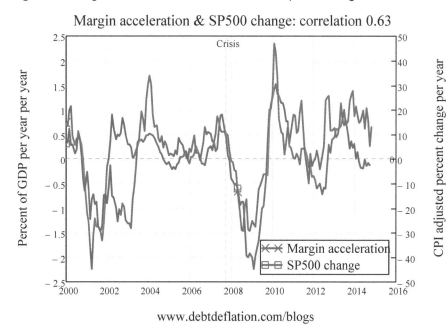

www.debtdeflation.com/blogs

Developing an economics for the post-crisis world

Economists have no ears (July, 2001)

Thomas Kuhn once famously described textbooks as the vehicle by which students learn how to do "normal science" in an academic discipline. Economic textbooks clearly fulfil this function, but the pity is that what passes for "normal" in economics barely deserves the appellation "science".

Most introductory economics textbooks present a sanitised, uncritical rendition of conventional economic theory, and the courses in which these textbooks are used do little to counter this mendacious presentation. Students might learn, for example, that "externalities" reduce the efficiency of the market mechanism. However, they will not learn that the "proof" that markets are efficient is itself flawed.

Since this textbook rendition of economics is also profoundly boring, the majority of those exposed to introductory course in economics do no more than this, and instead go on to careers in accountancy, finance or management – in which, nonetheless, many continue to harbour the simplistic notions they were taught many years earlier.

The minority which continues on to further academic training is taught the complicated techniques of economic analysis, with little to no discussion of whether these techniques are actually intellectually valid. The enormous critical literature is simply left out of advanced courses, while glaring logical shortcomings are glossed over with specious assumptions. However, most students accept these assumptions because their training leaves them both insufficiently literate and insufficiently numerate.

Most modern-day economics students are insufficiently literate because economic education eschews the study of the history of economic thought. Even a passing acquaintance with this literature exposes the reader to critical perspectives on conventional economic theory – but students today receive no such exposure.

They are insufficiently numerate because the material which establishes the intellectual weaknesses of economics is complex. Understanding this literature in its raw form requires an appreciation of some quite difficult areas of mathematics-concepts which require up to two years of undergraduate mathematical training to understand.

Curiously, though economists like to intimidate other social scientists with the mathematical rigour of their discipline, most economists do not have this level of mathematical education. Though economics students do attend numerous courses on mathematics, these are normally given by other economists. The argument for this approach – the partially sighted leading the partially sighted – is that generalist mathematics courses don't teach the concepts needed to understand mathematical economics (or the economic version of statistics, known as econometrics). As any student of econometrics knows, this is quite often true. However, it has the side effect that economics has persevered with mathematical methods which professional mathematicians have long ago transcended. This dated version of mathematics shields students from new developments in mathematics that, incidentally, undermine much of neoclassical economic theory.

One example of this is the way economists have reacted to "chaos theory". Most economists think that chaos theory has had little or no impact-which is generally true in economics, but not at all true in most other sciences. This is partially because, to understand chaos theory, you have to understand an area of mathematics known as "ordinary differential equations". Yet this topic is taught in very few courses on mathematical economics - and where it is taught, it is not covered in sufficient depth.

Students may learn some of the basic techniques for handling linear difference or differential equations, but chaos and complexity only begin to manifest themselves in non-linear difference and differential equations". A student in a conventional "quantitative methods in economics" subject will thus acquire the prejudices that "dynamics is uninteresting", which is largely true of the behaviour of linear dynamical systems, but not at all true of non-linear systems. This prejudice then isolates the student from much of what is new and interesting in mathematical theory and practice, let alone from what scientists in other sciences are doing.

Economists have no ears

Economics students therefore graduate from Masters and PhD programs with an effectively vacuous understanding of economics, no appreciation of the intellectual history of their discipline, and an approach to mathematics which hobbles both their critical understanding of economics, and their ability to appreciate the latest advances in mathematics and other sciences.

A minority of these ill-informed students themselves go on to be academic economists, and then repeat the process. Ignorance is perpetuated.

The attempt to conduct a critical dialogue within the profession of academic economics has therefore failed, not because economics has no flaws, but because – figuratively speaking – conventional economists have no ears. So then, "No More Mr Nice Guy". If economists can't be trusted to follow the Queensberry Rules of intellectual debate, then we critics have to step out of the boxing ring and into the streets. Hence my book "Debunking Economics", which describes the many formal academic critiques of neoclassical economics in a manner which –I hope – is accessible to the interested non-economist and non-mathematical readership. But it should also prove very useful to those who have come to regard conventional economic theory as autistic, since it clearly and simply explains the source of this endemic autism.

Developing an economics for the post-crisis world

Mad, bad, and dangerous to know

The most important thing that global financial crisis has done for economic theory is to show that neoclassical economics is not merely wrong, but dangerous.

Neoclassical economics contributed directly to this crisis by promoting a faith in the innate stability of a market economy, in a manner which in fact increased the tendency to instability of the financial system. With its false belief that all instability in the system can be traced to interventions in the market, rather than the market itself, it championed the deregulation of finance and a dramatic increase in income inequality. Its equilibrium vision of the functioning of finance markets led to the development of the very financial products that are now threatening the continued existence of capitalism itself.

Simultaneously it distracted economists from the obvious signs of an impending crisis – the asset market bubbles, and above all the rising private debt that was financing them. Paradoxically, as capitalism's "perfect storm" approached, neoclassical macroeconomists were absorbed in smug self-congratulation over their apparent success in taming inflation and the trade cycle, in what they termed "The Great Moderation". Ben Bernanke's contribution to this is worth quoting at length:

> ... the low-inflation era of the past two decades has seen not only significant improvements in economic growth and productivity but also a marked reduction in economic volatility..., a phenomenon that has been dubbed "the Great Moderation". Recessions have become less frequent and milder, and... volatility in output and employment has declined significantly... The sources of the Great Moderation remain somewhat controversial, but... there is evidence for the view that improved control of inflation has contributed in

important measure to this welcome change in the economy... Bernanke, 2004 (federalreserve.gov/boarddocs/speeches/2004/20041008/default.htm).

It is all very well to have economic theory dominated by a school of thought with an innate faith in the stability of markets when those markets are forever gaining – whether by growth in the physical economy, or via rising prices in the asset markets. In those circumstances, academic economists aligned to PAECON can rail about the logical inconsistencies in mainstream economics all they want: they will be, and were, ignored by government, the business community, and most of the public, because their concerns don't appear to matter.

They can even be put down as critics of capitalism – worse still, as proponents of socialism – because it seems to those outside academia, and to neoclassical economists as well, that what they are attacking is not economic theory, but capitalism itself: "You think markets are unstable? Shame on you!"

The story is entirely different when asset markets crash beneath a mountain of debt, and the ensuing fallout threatens to take the physical economy with it. Now it should be possible to have the critics of neoclassical economics appreciated for what we really are: critics of a fundamentally false theory of the operations of a market economy, and tentative developers of a new, realistic analysis of the nature of capitalism, warts and all.

Changing pedagogy

Given how severe this crisis has already proven to be, the reform of economic theory and education should be an easy and urgent task. But that is not how things will pan out. Though the "irresistible force" of the Global Financial Crisis is indeed immense, so too is the inertia of the "immovable object" of economic belief.

Mad, bad, and dangerous to know

Despite the severity of the crisis in the real world, academic neoclassical economists will continue to teach from the same textbooks in 2009 and 2010 that they used in 2008 and earlier (laziness will be as influential a factor here as ideological commitment). Rebel economists will be emboldened to proclaim "I told you so" in their non-core subjects, but in the core micro, macro and finance units, it will be business as usual virtually everywhere. Many undergraduate economics students in the coming years will sit gobsmacked. As their lecturers recite textbook theory as if there is nothing extraordinarily different taking place in the real economy.

The same will happen in the academic journals. The editors of the *American Economic Review* and the *Economic Journal* are unlikely to convert to Post-Keynesian or Evolutionary Economics or Econophysics any time soon – let alone to be replaced by editors who are already practitioners of non-orthodox thought. The battle against neoclassical economic orthodoxy within universities will be long and hard, even though its failure will be apparent to those in the non-academic world.

Much of this will be because neoclassical economists are genuinely naïve about their role in causing this crisis. From their perspective, they will interpret the crisis as due to poor regulation, and to government intervention in areas that should have been left to the market. Aspects of the crisis that cannot be solely attributed to those causes will be covered by appealing to embellishments to basic neoclassical theory. Thus, for example, the Subprimes Scam will be portrayed as something easily explained by the theory of asymmetric information.

They will seriously believe that the crisis calls not for the abolition of neoclassical economics, but for its teachings to be more widely known. The very thought that this financial crisis should require any change in what they do, let alone necessitate the rejection of neoclassical theory completely, will strike them as incredible.

In this sense, they are like the Maxwellian physicists about whom Max Planck remarked that

"A new scientific truth does not triumph by convincing its opponents and making them see the light, but rather because its opponents eventually die, and a new generation grows up that is familiar with it" (Kuhn 1970, p. 150).

But physics is charmed in comparison to economics, since it is inherently an empirical discipline, and quantum mechanics gave the only explanation to the empirically quantifiable black body problem. Planck's confidence that a new generation would take the place of the old was therefore well-founded. But in economics, not only will the neoclassical old guard resist change, they could, if economic circumstances stabilise, give rise to a new generation that accepts their interpretation of the crisis. This is how the success of the Keynesian counter-revolution came about, and it is why we have we entered this crisis with an even more rabid neoclassicism than confronted Keynes in the 1930s.

The first thing that the global financial crisis should therefore do to economics is to galvanise student protest about the lack of debate within academic economics itself, because dissident academic economists will be unable to shift the tuition of economics themselves without massive pressure from the student body.

I speak from my own experience, when I was one of many students who agitated against neoclassical economics in the early 1970s at Sydney University, and campaigned for the establishment of a Political Economy Department. Were it not for the protests by the students against what we then rightly saw as a deluded approach to economics, the non-neoclassical staff at Sydney University would have been unable to affect change themselves.

Though we won that battle at Sydney University, we lost the war. The economic downturn of the mid-1970s allowed for the defeat of what Joan Robinson aptly called the Bastard Keynesianism of that era, and its replacement by Friedman's "monetarism". Our protests were also wrongly characterised as being essentially anti-capitalist. Though there were indeed many who were anti-capitalist within the Political Economy movement, the real target of student protest was a poor theory of how capitalism operates, and not capitalism itself.

Similar observations can be made about the PAECON movement today, where student dissatisfaction with neoclassical economics in France spilled over into a worldwide movement. Though the initial impact of the movement was substantial, neoclassical dominance of economic pedagogy continued unabated. The movement persisted, but its relevance to the real economy was not appreciated because that economy appeared to be booming. Now that the global economy is in crisis, student pressure is needed once more to ensure that, this time, real change to economic pedagogy occurs.

Business pressure is also essential. Business groups to some degree naively believed that those who proclaimed the virtues of the market system, and who argued on their side in disputes over income distribution, were their allies in the academy, while critics of the market were their enemies. I hope that this financial catastrophe will convince the business community that its true friends in the academy are those who understand the market system, whether they criticise or praise it. As much as we need students to revolt over the teaching of economics, we need business to bring pressure on academic economics departments to revise their curricula because of the financial crisis.

Changing economics

The pedagogic pressure from students and the wider community has to be matched by the accelerated development of alternatives to neoclassical economics. Though we know much more today about the innate flaws in neoclassical thought than was known at the time of the Great Depression (Keen 2001), the development of a fully-fledged alternative to it is still a long way off. There are multiple alternative schools of thought extant – from Post Keynesian to Evolutionary and Behavioural Economics, and Econophysics – but these are not developed enough to provide a fully-fledged alternative to neoclassical economics.

This should not dissuade us from dispensing completely with the neoclassical approach. For some substantial period, and especially while the actual economy remains in turmoil, we have to accept a period of turmoil in the teaching of and research into economics. Hanging on to parts of a failed paradigm simply because it has components that other schools lack would be a tragic mistake, because it is from precisely such relics that a neoclassical vision could once again become dominant when – or rather if – the market economy emerges from this crisis.

Key here should be a rejection of neoclassical microeconomics in its entirety. This was the missing component of Keynes's revolution. While he tried to overthrow macroeconomics shibboleths like Say's Law, he continued to accept not merely the microeconomic concepts such as perfect competition, but also their unjustified projection into macroeconomic areas – as with his belief that the marginal productivity theory of income distribution, which is fundamentally a micro concept, applied at the macro level of wage determination.

From this failure to expunge the microeconomic foundations of neoclassical economics from post-Great Depression economics arose the "microfoundations of macroeconomics" debate that led ultimately to rational expectations representative agent macroeconomics, in which the economy is modelled as a single utility maximising individual who is blessed with perfect knowledge of the future.

Fortunately, behavioural economics provides the beginnings of an alternative vision as to how individuals operate in a market environment, while multi-agent modelling and network theory give us foundations for understanding group dynamics in a complex society. They explicitly emphasise what neoclassical economics has evaded: that aggregation of heterogeneous individuals results in emergent properties of the group which cannot be reduced to the behaviour of any "representative individual" amongst them. These approaches should replace neoclassical microeconomics completely.

The changes to economic theory beyond the micro level involve a complete recanting of the neoclassical vision. The vital first step here is to abandon the obsession with equilibrium.

The fallacy that dynamic processes must be modelled as if the system is in continuous equilibrium through time is probably the most important reason for the intellectual failure of neoclassical economics. Mathematics, sciences and engineering long ago developed tools to model out of equilibrium processes, and this dynamic approach to thinking about the economy should become second nature to economists.

An essential pedagogic step here is to hand the teaching of mathematical methods in economics over to mathematics departments. Any mathematical training in economics, if it occurs at all, should come *after* students have done at least basic calculus, algebra and differential equations – the last area being one about which most economists of all persuasions are woefully ignorant. This simultaneously explains why neoclassical economists obsess too much about proofs, and why non-neoclassical economists like those in the Circuit School (Graziani 1989) have had such difficulties in translating excellent verbal ideas about credit creation into coherent dynamic models of a monetary production economy (c.f. Keen 2009).

Neoclassical economics has effectively insulated itself from the great advances made in these genuine sciences and engineering in the last forty years, so that while its concepts appear difficult, they are quaint in comparison to the sophistication evident today in mathematics, engineering, computing, evolutionary biology and physics. This isolation must end, and for a substantial while economics must eat humble pie and learn from these disciplines that it has for so long studiously ignored. Some researchers from those fields have called for the wholesale replacement of standard economics curricula with at least the building blocks of modern thought in these disciplines, and in the light of the catastrophe economists have visited upon the real world, their arguments carry substantial weight.

For example, in response to a paper critical of trends in econophysics (Gallegatti et al. 2006), the physicist Joe McCauley responded that, though some of the objections were valid, the problems in economics proper were far worse. He therefore suggested that:

> the economists revise their curriculum and require that the following topics be taught: calculus through the advanced level, ordinary differential equations (including advanced), partial differential equations (including Green functions), classical mechanics through modern nonlinear dynamics, statistical physics, stochastic processes (including solving Smoluchowski – Fokker – Planck equations), computer programming (C, Pascal, etc.) and, for complexity, cell biology. *Time for such classes can be obtained in part by eliminating micro- and macro-economics classes from the curriculum.* The students will then face a much harder curriculum, and those who survive will come out ahead. So might society as a whole (McCauley 2006, p. 608; emphasis added).

The economic theory that should eventually emerge from the rejection of neoclassical economics and the basic adoption of dynamic methods will come much closer than neoclassical economics could ever do to meeting Marshall's dictum that "The Mecca of the economist lies in economic biology rather than in economic dynamics" (Marshall 1920: xiv). As Veblen correctly surmised over a century ago (Veblen 1898), the failure of economics to become an evolutionary science is the product of the optimising framework of the underlying paradigm, which is inherently antithetical to the process of evolutionary change. This reason, above all others, is why the neoclassical mantra that the economy must be perceived as the outcome of the decisions of utility maximising individuals must be rejected.

Economics also has to become fundamentally a monetary discipline, right from the consideration of how individuals make market decisions through to our understanding of macroeconomics. The myth of "the money illusion" (which can only be true in a world without debt) has to be dispelled from day one, while our macroeconomics has to be that of a monetary economy in which nominal magnitudes matter – precisely because they are the link between the value of current output and the financing of accumulated debt.

Mad, bad, and dangerous to know

The dangers of excessive debt and deflation simply cannot be comprehended from a neoclassical perspective, which – along with the inability to reason outside the confines of equilibrium – explains the profession's failure to assimilate Fisher's prescient warnings (Fisher, 1933; "few people realise that Friedman's preferred rate of inflation in his "Optimum Quantity of Money" paper was 'a *decline* in prices at the rate of at least 5 per cent per year, and perhaps decidedly more'; Friedman 1969, p. 46, emphasis added").

The discipline must also become fundamentally empirical, in contrast to the faux empiricism of econometrics. By this I mean basing itself on the economic and financial data first and foremost – the collection and interpretation of which has been the hallmark of contributions by econophysicists – and by respecting economic history, a topic that has been expunged from economics departments around the world. It, along with a non-Whig approach to the history of economic thought, should be restored to the economics curriculum. Names that currently are absent from modern economics courses (Marx, Veblen, Keynes, Fisher, Kalecki, Schumpeter, Minsky, Sraffa, Goodwin, to name a few) should abound in such courses.

Ironically, one of the best calls for a focus on the empirical data *sans* a preceding economic model came from two of the most committed neoclassical authors, 2004 Nobel Prize winners Finn Kydland and Edward Prescott, when they noted that "the reporting of facts – without assuming the data are generated by some probability model – is an important scientific activity. We see no reason for economics to be an exception" (Kydland & Prescott 1990, p. 3). The failure of these authors to live up to their own standards[1] should not be replicated in post-neoclassical economics.

---

[1] See Prescott 1999, in which he blamed the Great Depression on "a great decline in steady-state market hours" which was "the unintended consequence of labor market institutions and industrial policies designed to improve the performance of the economy", though he was unable to specify what these were: "Exactly what changes in market institutions and industrial policies gave rise to the large decline in normal market hours is not clear" (Prescott 1999, p. 29).

References

Irving Fisher, (1933). "The debt-deflation theory of great depressions", *Econometrica*, Vol. 1, pp. 337-357.

Milton Friedman, (1969), *The Optimum Quantity of Money and Other Essays*, Macmillan, Chicago.

Mauro Gallegatti, Steve Keen, Thomas Lux & Paul Ormerod (2006). "Worrying Trends in Econophysics", *Physica A* Vol. 370, pp. 1-6.

Graziani Augusto, (1989). "The Theory of the Monetary Circuit", *Thames Papers in Political Economy*, Spring, pp. 1-26. Reprinted in M. Musella and C. Panico (eds) (1995). *The Money Supply in the Economic Process*, Edward Elgar, Aldershot.

Steve Keen, (2001). *Debunking Economics: the naked emperor of the social sciences*, Pluto Press & Zed Books, Sydney & London; http://www.mobipocket.com/en/eBooks/BookDetails.asp?BookID=131405&Origine=4965

Steve Keen, (2009). "Bailing out the Titanic with a Thimble", *Economic Analysis and Policy*, Vol. 39 Issue 1; www.eap-journal.com.au

Thomas Kuhn, (1962). *The Structure of Scientific Revolutions*, University Of Chicago Press, Chicago.

Finn E. Kydland and Edward C. Prescott, (1990). "Business Cycles: Real Facts and a Monetary Myth", *Federal Reserve Bank of Minneapolis Quarterly Review*, Vol. 23, no. 1, pp. 3–19.

Joseph L. McCauley (2006). "Response to "Worrying Trends in Econophysics"", *Physica A* 371, pp. 601–609.

Alfred Marshall, (1920). *Principles of Economics, 9th Edition*, Macmillan, London.

Edward C. Prescott (1999). "Some Observations on the Great Depression", *Federal Reserve Bank of Minneapolis Quarterly Review*, Vol. 23, pp. 25–31.

Thorstein Veblen, (1898). "Why is Economics not an Evolutionary Science?", The Quarterly Journal of Economics, pp. 373-397.

Debunking the theory of the firm
– a chronology
Steve Keen and Russell Standish

A personal introduction by Steve Keen

I have been an economics renegade for almost 40 years, and for most of that time I have had to tolerate neoclassical economists either dismissing my work or ignoring it. Since the Global Financial Collapse began, that has ceased to be the case. Neoclassical economists, although hardly likely to become born-again Post Keynesians, are chastened and to some degree humbled by their inability to anticipate this crisis. Moreover, it's hard for them to hide behind the "Black Swans" defence when the speaker is someone credited with having predicted the crisis before it happened.

So that's all and good; one might even think that the seeds have been laid to finally achieve a true reform of economics, to make it empirical rather than a priori.

However, one also notices a worrying trend among neoclassicals today. True, after having had their macroeconomics lambasted and having been shown how Minsky's analysis makes sense of what they can't understand, they are often willing to admit that neoclassical macroeconomics is a shambles. No-one, they will say, defends rational expectations anymore. But then they assert: *at least neoclassical microeconomics is sound.*

This is patently absurd – especially since neoclassical macro was built largely by subverting its "Keynesian" predecessor on the grounds that it "did not have good microfoundations", and then casting macroeconomics as applied neoclassical microeconomics. However, despite this, neoclassicals still cling to the purity of their vision of the utility maximising consumer on one side of the market, and the profit-maximising firm on the other.

But absurd though it may be, it is an echo of what happened when Keynes tried to bring economics into the real world eighty years ago. Led by Hicks, Samuelson and the like, the neoclassicals dragged the profession back into fantasy via their vision of a beautiful microeconomics.

For society's sake we need to prevent this intellectually reactionary behavior from being repeated after this crisis. A dispassionate analysis of neoclassical microeconomics shows that it is absurd on its own grounds – that, to coin a phrase "neoclassical microeconomics lacks good microeconomic foundations". But the superficial elegance of the theory remains seductive, and when nations have got beyond this crisis, the same seductive superficiality could give rise to a neoclassical resurgence.

It therefore seems extremely important to emphasize and demonstrate again that their microeconomics is irreparably flawed. This was the task of my book *Debunking Economics*: to point out that, for example "downward-sloping market demand curves" don't slope downwards unless there is just one consumer and one commodity (the Sonnenschein-Mantel-Debreu conditions, treated properly as a proof by contradiction that individual demand curves can't be aggregated), that a marginal product of capital can't be defined (Sraffa's critique), and so on.

In most of *Debunking Economics*, I simply repackaged established critiques by previous authors – I stood on the shoulders of the giants that neoclassical economics ignored. But there was one part of the theory that, when I began the book, simply appeared irrelevant rather than analytically false: the theory of the firm. From my own experience as a young believer in mainstream economics, I realised how powerful that vision of intersecting supply and demand curves in a competitive, efficient market is, but all I could do, I thought, was parody its irrelevance rather than analytically dismiss it.

Then I spotted a flaw that, to my knowledge at the time, had not been noted before: that the assumptions of a downward sloping market demand curve and a horizontal firm demand curve in the perfectly competitive model were mutually incompatible.

I since have discovered that I wasn't the first to point this out – Stigler, of all people, had done it in 1957. But I added a proof that what neoclassical economics calls profit-maximising behaviour – equating marginal cost and marginal revenue – provably does not maximise profits.

Further analysis found many other flaws in the superficially seductive "logic" of the neoclassical theory of the firm. In many ways, the flaws in this crucial part of neoclassical microeconomics are worse, and more easily proven, than those in consumer theory or capital theory or the like.

Of course, attempts to get this analysis published in mainstream economic journals prior to 2008 predictably failed; my various papers appeared in non-mainstream books and journals, and even the journal of interdisciplinary physics, *Physica A*.

I was content to leave them there and focus on my main interest today, of extending Minsky's work to understand the financial crisis. But then Australia's Treasury drafted a new tax whose foundation was the intellectually flawed vision of a competitive market, with firms facing a horizontal demand curve, and profit-maximising by equating marginal cost and marginal revenue.

So I decided to put together this compendium of all the reasons why this widely believed theory is nonsense. I start with the simplest disproofs that I have developed, and progress right through to a critique of Cournot-Nash theory. It's heavy going, but I fear that unless we really drive a stake through the heart of this vampire logic called neoclassical economics, it will rise again and lead us back to ignorance once we forget the Global Financial Collapse, as our predecessors forgot the Great Depression.

Stigler 1957

The proposition that Keen had thought original in *Debunking Economics* – that, under conditions of "atomism", the slope of the demand curve facing the individual competitive firm was the same as the slope of the market demand curve – had in fact been made in 1957 by that arch defender of neoclassicism, George Stigler, and in a leading neoclassical journal: *The Journal of Political Economy* (Stigler 1957 – see Figure 8).

Figure 8: Stigler 1957

THE JOURNAL OF
POLITICAL ECONOMY

Volume LXV	FEBRUARY 1957	Number 1

PERFECT COMPETITION, HISTORICALLY CONTEMPLATED

GEORGE J. STIGLER

[31] Let one seller dispose of q_i, the other sellers each disposing of q. Then the seller's marginal revenue is

$$\frac{d\,(p\,q_i)}{d\,q_i} = p + q_i\,\frac{dp}{dQ}\,\frac{dQ}{d\,q_i},$$

where Q is total sales, and $dQ/dq_i = 1$. Letting $Q = nq_i = nq$, and writing E for

$$\frac{dQ}{dp}\,\frac{p}{Q},$$

we obtain the expression in the text.

Stigler's simple application of the chain rule showed that the underlying assumption of the Marshallian model – atomism, that firms in a competitive industry do not react strategically to the hypothetical actions of other firms – is incompatible with each firm facing a horizontal demand curve. In an n firm industry where the output of the ith firm is q_i, this assumption, means that:

$$\frac{\partial q_i}{\partial q_j} = 0 \; \forall i \neq j$$

As a result

$$\frac{dQ}{dq_i} = 1$$

and hence

$$\frac{dP}{dq_i} = \frac{dP}{dQ} :$$

$$\frac{dP}{dq_i} = \frac{dP}{dQ}\frac{dQ}{dq_i}$$

$$= \frac{dP}{dQ}\left(\sum_{j=1}^{n} \frac{\partial q_j}{\partial q_i} \right) \qquad\qquad 1.5$$

$$= \frac{dP}{dQ}\left(\frac{\partial q_i}{\partial q_i} + \sum_{j \neq i}^{n} \frac{\partial q_j}{\partial q_i} \right)$$

$$= \frac{dP}{dQ}\left(1 + \sum_{j \neq i}^{n} 0 \right)$$

$$= \frac{dP}{dQ}$$

It is thus impossible for the market demand function $P(Q)$, where $Q = \sum_{i=1}^{n} q_i$, to have the dual properties that $P'(Q) < 0$ and $P'(q_i) = 0$ – and Stigler had shown this in 1957! Yet the claim that the market demand curve is negatively sloped, while the individual perfectly competitive firm faces a horizontal demand curve, has graced the opening chapters of every economics textbook published in the last half century.

Mendacity in education – another personal observation

One of my motivations for writing *Debunking Economics* was my belief that an education in economics was mendacious. I had in mind the failure to note the Cambridge Controversy arguments when discussing the concept of an aggregate production function (see Chapter 6 of Debunking Economics), or the avoidance of the Sonnenschein-Mantel-Debreu conditions when deriving a market demand curve from the aggregation of individual ones (Chapter 2).

When I discussed these issues with any of the minority of neoclassical economists who were themselves aware of those critiques, the even smaller minority who did not dismiss them outright would raise the pedagogic defense of difficulty. These topics are complex, and require an advanced knowledge, not only of economics, but of mathematics. Better to give new students a simple introduction – well behaved aggregate production functions, nice downward sloping market demand curves, and so on – and cover the nuances when they have more knowledge.

No such defense applies here: the only mathematical knowledge needed to comprehend that Marshallian atomism is incompatible with a horizontal demand curve for the firm is elementary calculus.

The responses I have received on this point from neoclassical economists to date have been disingenuous. At best, they have referred to Stigler's attempt to recast perfect competition as the limiting case as the number of firms in an industry increases (discussed in the next section).[2] At worst, they have claimed that the laws of mathematics do not apply to economics.[3]

---

[2] A referee for the *Economic Journal* wrote that "we always consider the perfect competition case as a polar case which represents an extreme scenario, and is largely a benchmark. I would prefer to see the equation: (AR - MR)/AR = 1 /(nE), so that for E at a normal value of say 2, and n at 1000, then the divergence of AR and MR is $1/20^t$ of 1%. Then price equals MR seems a pretty good approximation!"

[3] A referee for the *Journal of Economic Education* commented that "Stigler's many attempts to save neoclassical theory have always caused more problems than they have solved. His version of the chain rule is contrary to the partial equilibrium method and thus is irrelevant".

The latter claim is of course nonsense for an approach to economics which, from its founding father to today's leading exponents, exalted itself over its rivals because it *was* mathematical:

> ... those economists who do not know any mathematics ... can never prevent the theory of the determination of prices under free competition from becoming a mathematical theory. Hence, they will always have to face the alternative either of steering clear of this discipline ... or of tackling the problems of pure economics without the necessary equipment, thus producing not only very bad pure economics but also very bad mathematics (Walras 1900 [1954]: 47).

This raises the question of why neoclassical economists defend commencing an education in economics with such bad mathematics? We expect it is because the fantasy of perfect competition is essential to fulfilling the vision of rational self-interested behavior being compatible with welfare maximization. If one admits that the individual firm faces a downward-sloping demand curve, then the elimination of deadweight loss that is the hallmark of perfect competition can't possibly be compatible with individual profit-maximization.

This is easily illustrated using another standard mathematical technique, the Taylor series expansion.[4]

Perfect competitors aren't profit maximizers

Consider a competitive industry where all firms are producing at the "perfect competition" level where price equals marginal cost. In general, profit for the ith firm is:

$$\pi_i(q_i) = P(Q) \cdot q_i - TC(q_i) \tag{1.6}$$

---

[4] This proof was first developed by John Legge, of La Trobe University.

What happens to the ith firm's profits if it changes its output by a small amount q_i ? Under the Marshallian condition of atomism, industry output also changes by the same amount. The change in profit $\delta\pi\,(\delta q_i)$ is thus:

$$\pi_i\left(q_i+\delta q_i\right)-\pi_i\left(q_i\right)=\left(P\left(Q+\delta q_i\right)\cdot\left(q_i+\delta q_i\right)-TC\left(q_i+\delta q_i\right)\right)-\left(P\left(Q\right)\cdot q_i-TC\left(q_i\right)\right)$$
(1.7)

This can be approximated by applying the first order Taylor series expansion, and by making the substitution that, at this output level, price equals marginal cost: $P(Q)=TC'(q_i)$. The symbolic mathematics engine in Mathcad makes fast work of this approximation:[5]

Figure 9: Mathcad's symbolic solution for change in a firm's profit from perfect competition output level

$$\left[P\left(Q+\delta q_i\right)\cdot\left(q_i+\delta q_i\right)-TC\left(q_i+\delta q_i\right)\right]-\left(P(Q)\cdot q_i-TC\left(q_i\right)\right) \quad \begin{vmatrix} \text{expand} \\ \text{series}, \delta q_i, 1 \\ \text{substitute}, \dfrac{d}{dq_i}TC\left(q_i\right)=P(Q) \end{vmatrix}$$

$$\rightarrow q_i\cdot\delta q_i\cdot\frac{d}{dQ}P(Q)$$

Therefore:

$$\delta\pi\left(\delta q_i\right)\approx q_i\cdot\delta q_i\cdot\frac{d}{dQ}P$$

.

---

[5] We are using a symbolic mathematics program both to reduce the need for some tedious manual calculations, and because on several occasions, neoclassical economists have disputed the results of manual calculations – by in effect distorting the definition of a derivative.

Since $\frac{d}{dQ}P < 0$, if $\delta q_i < 0$ – if, in words, the firm reduces its output – its profit will rise. Thus the output level at which price equals marginal cost is not a profit maximum for the individual competitive firm, and if such a firm is indeed a profit maximizer, it will reduce its output below this level.

Some neoclassical economists have thrown the "perfect knowledge" assumption at us at this point: perfectly informed consumers will instantly stop buying from the firm that has reduced its output and increased its price, and switch to those that are still setting price equal to marginal cost. But this argument is still based on the "horizontal demand curve" assumption, which itself is a furphy,[6] and the market price in the model has already risen because of the change in output by one firm – there is no "cheaper supplier" to whom omniscient consumers can turn.

"Price equals marginal cost" is, therefore, not an equilibrium under the Marshallian assumption of atomism. As a result, the coincidence of collective welfare and the pursuit of individual profit is impossible: if neoclassical economists want to pull that particular rabbit out of a hat, they need another hat. Stigler attempted to provide one.

Stigler's limiting case

Stigler, of course, was not trying to bury perfect competition when he showed that:

$$\frac{dP}{dq_i} = \frac{dP}{dQ}$$

he was one of the pre-eminent defenders of the neoclassical model against empirically-oriented researchers like Eiteman and Means (see Freedman 1998). He therefore devised an alternative explanation of perfect competition, as the limiting case of competition as the number of firms in an

---

[6] "Furphy" is a delightful Australian word meaning "an irrelevant or minor issue raised to specifically divert attention away from the real issue". It deserves wider currency – especially amongst economists!

Developing an economics for the post-crisis world

industry increased. His analysis, shown in Figure 8, footnoted the derivation of the expression shown in Figure 10.

Figure 10: Stigler's expression for marginal revenue (Stigler 1957: 8)

$$\text{Marginal revenue} = \text{Price}$$
$$+ \frac{\text{Price}}{\text{Number of sellers} \times \text{Market elasticity}}$$

Stigler then asserted that "this last term goes to zero as the number of sellers increases indefinitely" (Stigler 1957: 8). Marginal revenue for the ith firm thus converges to market price. Perfect competition thus appeared to be saved, despite a downward-sloping firm's demand curve: profit-maximizers would set marginal cost equal to marginal revenue, and this would converge to price as more firms entered a market.

Stigler's convergence argument is technically correct, but in conflict with the proof shown above that "price equals marginal cost" is *not* a profit maximum for the individual firm. The resolution of this conflict led to Keen's first truly original contribution to this literature: *the proposition that equating marginal revenue and marginal cost maximizes profit is also a furphy.*

Equating MC and MR doesn't maximize profits

Generations of economists have been taught the simple mantra that "profit is maximized by equating marginal cost and marginal revenue". The proof simply differentiates (1.6) with respect to q_i. However, the individual firm's profit is a function, not only of its own output, but of that of all other firms in the industry. This is true regardless of whether the firm reacts strategically to what other firms do, and regardless of whether it can control what other firms do. The objectively true profit maximum is therefore given by the zero of the *total* differential: the differential of the firm's profit with respect to total industry output.

Debunking the theory of the firm – a chronology

We stress that this issue is independent of whether the individual firm can or cannot work out this maximum for itself, whether the firm does or does not interact with its competitors, and whether the firm does or does not control the variables that determine the profit maximum. Given a mathematically specified market inverse demand function that is a function of the aggregate quantity supplied to the market, and a mathematically specified total cost function for the individual firm that is a function of its output, the question "what is the level of the firm's output that maximizes its profit?" is completely independent of the question of "will the firm, in any given environment, or following any given behavioral rule, actually determine or achieve this level?". That objective, profit-maximizing level is given by the zero of the *total* differential of profit:

$$\frac{d}{dQ}\pi(q_i) = \frac{d}{dQ}\big(P(Q)q_i - TC(q_i)\big) = 0$$

(1.8)

This total derivative is the sum of n partial derivatives in an n-firm industry:

$$\frac{d}{dQ}\pi(q_i) = \sum_{j=1}^{n}\left\{\left(\frac{\partial}{\partial q_j}\pi(q_i)\right)\cdot\frac{d}{dQ}q_j\right\}$$

(1.9)

In the Marshallian case, atomism lets us set:

$$\frac{d}{dQ}q_j = 1 \ \forall j$$

(we address the Cournot case in section 0). Expanding (1.9) yields

$$\frac{d}{dQ}\pi(q_i) = \sum_{j=1}^{n}\left(\frac{\partial}{\partial q_j}\big(P(Q)q_i - TC(q_i)\big)\right)$$

(1.10)

Continuing with the product rule, (1.10) can be expanded to:

$$\frac{d}{dQ}\pi(q_i) = \sum_{j=1}^{n}\left(P(Q)\frac{\partial}{\partial q_j}q_i + q_i \cdot \frac{\partial}{\partial q_j}P(Q) - \frac{\partial}{\partial q_j}TC(q_i)\right)$$

(1.11)

Under the Marshallian assumption of atomism, the first term in the summation in (1.11) is zero where $j \neq i$, and $P(Q)$ where $j = i$. The second term is equal to:

$$q_i \cdot \frac{d}{dQ}P(Q) \ \forall j$$

the third is zero where $j \neq i$, and equal to

$$\frac{d}{dq_i}TC(q_i)$$

(or marginal cost $MC(q_i)$) where $j = i$. Equation (1.11) thus reduces to:

$$\frac{d}{dQ}\pi(q_i) = P(Q) + n \cdot q_i \cdot \frac{d}{dQ}P(Q) - MC(q_i)$$

(1.12)

The true profit maximum—under the Marshallian condition of atomism—is thus given by equation (1.13):

$$\pi(q_i)_{max} : MC(q_i) = P + n \cdot q_i \cdot \frac{dP}{dQ}$$

(1.13)

The error in the standard "Marshallian" formula is now obvious: it omits the number of firms in the industry from the expression for the individual firm's marginal revenue. With this error corrected, the correct profit-maximizing rule for a competitive firm is very similar to that for a monopoly: set marginal cost equal to *industry level* marginal revenue.[7]

Monopoly, competition, profit and hyper-rationality

Neoclassical economics assumes that, given revenue and cost functions, there is some output level that will maximize profits, and another that will maximize social welfare (by eliminating deadweight loss).[8] The argument that the two coincide under perfect competition has been shown to be nonsense. So too is the argument that a single rational firm could work out the profit maximum, but a bunch of rational *non-interacting* firms couldn't, as the calculus in the previous section shows.

Of course, an objection can be made to the above mathematical logic that solving equation **Error! Reference source not found.** requires knowledge of the number of firms in the industry, which the individual competitive firm can't be assumed to have.[9] Here, we can turn Milton Friedman's methodological defense of the theory of the firm against itself. Friedman, as is well known, argued that while firms didn't in fact do calculus to work out their profit-maximizing output levels, we could model their behavior "as if" they did, because unless the behavior of businessmen in some way or other approximated behavior consistent with the maximization of returns, it seems unlikely that they would remain in business for long. (Friedman 1953: 22)

---

[7] Though not necessarily identical, since $n \cdot q_i$ only equals Q if $q_i = \frac{Q}{n} \; \forall i$. This impact of dispersal in firm size may explain some of the simulation results shown later.

[8] We use standard undergraduate terms here because the analysis we are challenging is, up to this point, that served up to undergraduates. We address game theoretic concepts later.

[9] Equation (1.9) can be put in another form which partly addresses this criticism, and also emphasizes the error in the conventional formula. The profit-maximizing level of output is not to equate firm-level marginal revenue and marginal cost, but to make the gap between them a fraction of the gap between price and marginal cost: $MR(q_i) - MC(q_i) = \frac{n-1}{n}(P - MC)$. The fraction tends to 1 as $n \to \infty$, so the more "competitive" an industry is, the easier it is to apply this formula.

We are not arguing that firms do the calculus to work out this profit-maximizing level either.[10] Instead, we are simply showing that the calculus *can* be done, and the profit-maximizing level is not the one asserted by neoclassical economists. However, it is possible now – in a way that wasn't possible in 1953 – to actually carry out Friedman's "billiard players" experiment. Citing him again:

Now, of course, businessmen do not actually and literally solve the system of simultaneous equations in terms of which the mathematical economist finds it convenient to express this hypothesis, any more than leaves or billiard players explicitly go through complicated mathematical calculations or falling bodies decide to create a vacuum. The billiard player, if asked how he decides where to hit the ball, may say that he "just figures it out" but then also rubs a rabbit's foot just to make sure; and the businessman may well say that he prices at average cost, with of course some minor deviations when the market makes it necessary. The one statement is about as helpful as the other, and neither is a relevant test of the associated hypothesis. (Friedman 1953: 22)

A "relevant test of the associated hypothesis" is to set up a virtual market that conforms to neoclassical assumptions – with a static downward sloping market demand curve, and given cost functions subject to diminishing marginal productivity, so that there is indeed a profit-maximizing level of output for each firm – and see what happens. Figure 11 shows a Mathcad program that implements this.[11]

---

[10] In fact, we argue later that the assumption that there is some profit-maximizing level for a firm is a furphy. The profit-maximizing strategy for actual firms is simply sell as much as possible, at the greatest expense where possible.

[11] The behavior modeled was deliberately made as simple as possible, to avoid the rejoinder that the results were the product of our algorithm rather than raw profit-motivated behavior. It could only have been simpler by having each firm vary its output by one unit at each time step – a modification which, as it happens, results in a much slower but absolute convergence to the Keen equilibrium.

Figure 11: Simulation of instrumental profit maximizers

$$\text{Firms} := \begin{array}{|l} \text{Seed(rand)} \\[4pt] \text{for } i \in \text{firms}_{min}, \text{firms}_{min} + \text{firms}_{steps} .. \text{firms}_{max} \\[4pt] \quad \begin{array}{|l} Q_0 \leftarrow \begin{array}{|l} \text{round}\left(\text{runif}\left(i, q_K(i), q_C(i)\right)\right) \quad \text{if } i > 1 \\[4pt] q_C(i) \quad \text{otherwise} \end{array} \\[10pt] P_0 \leftarrow \begin{array}{|l} P\left(\sum Q_0, a, b\right) \quad \text{if } i > 1 \\[6pt] P\left(q_C(i), a, b\right) \quad \text{otherwise} \end{array} \\[12pt] dq \leftarrow \begin{array}{|l} \text{round}\left(\text{rnorm}\left(i, 0, \dfrac{q_C(i)}{100}\right)\right) \quad \text{if } i > 1 \\[10pt] \dfrac{q_C(i)}{100} \quad \text{otherwise} \end{array} \\[14pt] \text{for } j \in 0.. \text{runs} - 1 \\[4pt] \quad \begin{array}{|l} Q_{j+1} \leftarrow Q_j + dq \\[4pt] P_{j+1} \leftarrow \begin{array}{|l} P\left(\sum Q_{j+1}, a, b\right) \quad \text{if } i > 1 \\[6pt] P\left(Q_{j+1}, a, b\right) \quad \text{otherwise} \end{array} \\[10pt] dq \leftarrow \overrightarrow{\left[\text{sign}\left[\left(P_{j+1} \cdot Q_{j+1} - P_j \cdot Q_j\right) - \left(\text{tc}\left(Q_{j+1}, i\right) - \text{tc}\left(Q_j, i\right)\right)\right] \cdot dq\right]} \\[6pt] F_{j, i-1} \leftarrow Q_j \end{array} \end{array} \\[6pt] F \end{array}$$

Working through the program line by line:

1. A random number generator is seeded
2. A *for* loop iterates from a minimum number to a maximum number of firms

41

3. If there is more than one firm in the industry, each firm is randomly allocated an initial output level. The amounts are uniformly distributed from a minimum of the Keen prediction for a profit-maximizing firm, q_K to a maximum of the neoclassical prediction q_C.

4. If there is only one firm in the industry, its output starts at the level predicted by the neoclassical model – which coincides with q_K.

5. An initial market price is set, based on the sum of initial outputs.

6. Line 6 sets the market price in the case of a monopoly.

7. Each firm is randomly allocated an amount by which it varies output. The distribution has a mean of zero and a standard deviation of 1% of the neoclassical prediction for a profit-maximizing firm's output (this is the last aspect of the program that involves probability).

8. Line 8 allocates a change amount of 1% of the predicted output for a monopoly.

9. A *for* loop iterates over a number of runs where each firm varies its output trying to increase its profit from the initial level.

10. Firstly each firm adds its change amount to its initial output. This is a vector operation: if there are 100 firms in the industry Q_0 is a vector with 100 initial output amounts, and *dq* is a vector with 100 (positive or negative) output changes.

11. A new market price is calculated on the basis of the new aggregate output level.

12. Line 12 again allows for a monopoly.

13. Each firm then calculates whether its profit has risen or fallen as a result of its change in output, and the collective impact of all the changes in output on the market price. If a firm finds that its profit has risen, it continues to change output in the same direction; if its profit has fall, it changes its output by the same amount but in the opposite direction.

14. Each step in the iteration is stored in a multi-dimensional array.[12]

15. The multidimensional array is returned by the program.

The program was run with identical cost functions for each firm, set up so that the market aggregate marginal cost curve was independent of the

---

[12] In effect, F is a matrix where the jth and i^{th} column contains the vector of outputs by an i-firm's industry at the jth iteration.

number of firms in the industry (we return to this issue in the Appendix). The number of firms was varied from 1 to 100. The eventual aggregate output at the end of 1000 iterations is shown n Figure 12, and the corresponding market price is shown in Figure 13, against the predictions of the Neoclassical and the Keen approach respectively.

Figure 12: Aggregate output

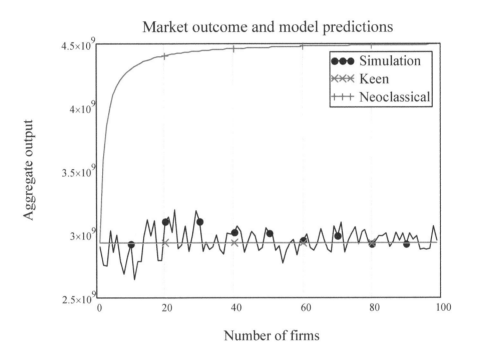

As is obvious, the number of firms in an industry had no impact on the eventual market output level or price: the Neoclassical prediction that price would converge to the level at which price equals marginal cost clearly was not fulfilled.

Figure 13: Market price

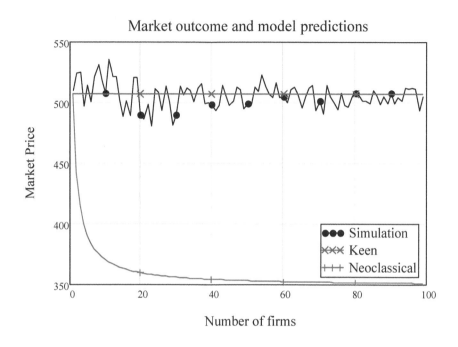

Some neoclassical referees thought that the results occurred because, though all firms were acting independently, they were all doing the same thing (reducing output from the initial level), and thus acting in a semi-collusive way.[13] In fact, as Figure 14 and Figure 15 show, though the average outcome conformed to Keen's predictions, the individual firms all pursued very different strategies. The aggregate outcome, which contradicted the neoclassical prediction and confirmed Keen's, was the result of quite diverse individual firm behavior – despite all firms having identical cost functions.

---

[13] A referee for the *Economic Journal* commented that "if firms act the same way, they will all get higher profits if and only if they reduce outputs. Then the algorithm will continue to lead them to the monopoly outcome since there is no chance any firm can realize the true impact of its own output change. Thus the result is not surprising."

Figure 14: Firm outputs in 100 firm industry

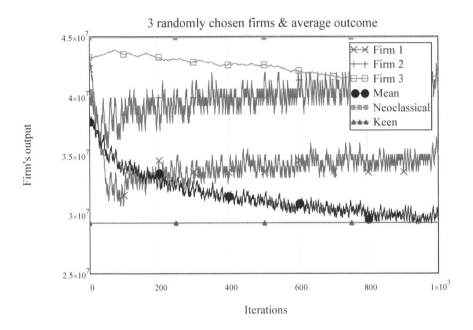

Figure 14 shows the output levels of 3 randomly chosen firms from the 100 firm industry, the average for all firms, and the predictions of the Keen and neoclassical formulae. Firm 1 began near the neoclassical output level, rapidly reduced output towards the "Keen" level, but then reversed direction; Firm 2 began halfway between the neoclassical and Keen predictions, then reduced output below the Keen level and stayed there; Firm 3 began closer to the neoclassical level and meandered closer to the Keen level.

The sole source of the volatility of each firm's behavior is the complex impact of interactions between firms, in the context of a very simply defined market – there is no random number generator causing this volatility. As Figure 15 shows, each firm made its changes in response to the impact of both its changes in output, and the collective changes in output, on its profit. Some firms made larger profits than others – notably the firms with the larger output made the larger profits. However, the average profit was much higher than predicted by the neoclassical model.

Figure 15: Firm profits in 100 firm industry

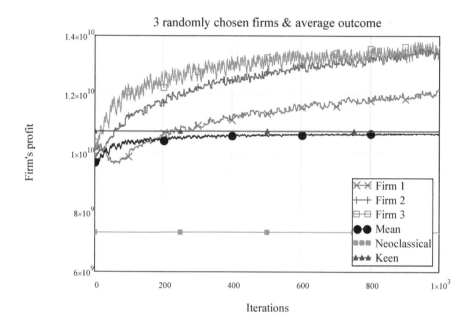

This model indicates that, in this game of competitive profit maximization, the virtual equivalents of Friedman's "billiard players" follow the laws of mathematics in their search for profits, as Friedman argued. However, these laws of mathematics are incompatible with the beliefs of neoclassical economists.

Since hyper-rational profit-maximizers cannot be relied upon to save neoclassical belief, there are only two avenues left: irrational behavior, and Cournot-Nash game theory.

Price-taking behavior is irrational

A regular neoclassical rejoinder to our analysis has been that we are "cheating" by not assuming rational, price-taking behavior. Our standard reply that the assumption of "price-taking" behavior is itself cheating, with regard to the laws of mathematics: as shown in Section 0, the assumption that $P'(q_i) = 0$ is incompatible with the assumption of a downward-sloping market demand curve $(P'(Q) < 0)$. However, it is also easily shown that "price-taking behavior" is irrational.

The assumption of price-taking behavior appears regularly in neoclassical economics, from the level of Marshallian analysis through to the foundations of general equilibrium analysis (see for example Mas-Colell et al 1995: 314, 383). Neoclassical economists do not seem to realize that this is a classic "rabbit in the hat" assumption: if it is assumed, then the "perfectly competitive" result of price equaling marginal cost follows, regardless of how many firms there are in the industry.

The essence of price-taking is the belief that a firm's change in its output doesn't affect market price: this amounts to setting

$$\frac{\partial}{\partial q_j} P(Q) = 0$$

in equation (1.11). This results in the "profit-maximizing strategy" of setting price equal to marginal cost, independently of the number of firms – that is, once this assumption is made, *even a monopoly produces where price equals marginal cost*. This behavior is clearly irrational for a monopoly, and it is only the "fog of large numbers" – the confusion of infinitesimals with zero, as Keen noted in *Debunking Economics* – that led neoclassical economists to regard price-taking as rational behavior for competitive firms.

Figure 16 illustrates that price-taking behavior is *irrational*: an agent who behaves this way is necessarily making a logical error. If the market demand curve slopes downwards, then the *a priori* rational belief is that *any* increase in output by the firm will depress market price.

Figure 16: Irrationality of "price-taking" behavior

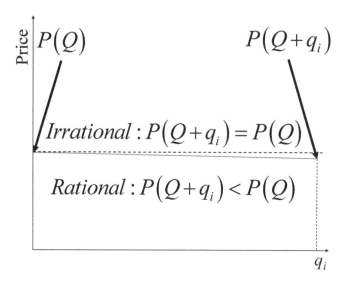

The desired neoclassical of price equal to marginal cost is thus dependent on irrational behavior (in the context of Marshallian competition – we address Cournot competition later). We quantify the degree of irrationality needed by modifying the program shown in Figure 11, so that a proportion of firms actually do behave irrationally: if a strategy has caused an increase in profit, a fraction of firms respond by *reversing* that strategy.

The modified program is shown in Figure 17. The outer loop (line 2) now iterates the counter i from 0 to 50, with the value representing the fraction of firms who behave irrationally at each iteration. The only change to the inner loop is that the change in output by each firm is now reversed for $i\%$ of firms at each iteration.[14]

---

[14] The function call $runif\left(firms, -i/100, -i/100+1\right)$ generates a vector of numbers between $-i/100$ and $1-i/100$; when $i=0$, all these numbers will be positive and thus not affect the value of the $sign()$ function; when $i>0$, $i\%$ of these numbers will be negative and thus the sign of the $sign()$ function will be reversed. The firms that have this randomly assigned negative number against their output change will increase output at the next step if profit rose when the decreased output on the previous step (and vice versa). This is instrumentally irrational behavior.

Figure 17: Analyzing the impact of irrationality

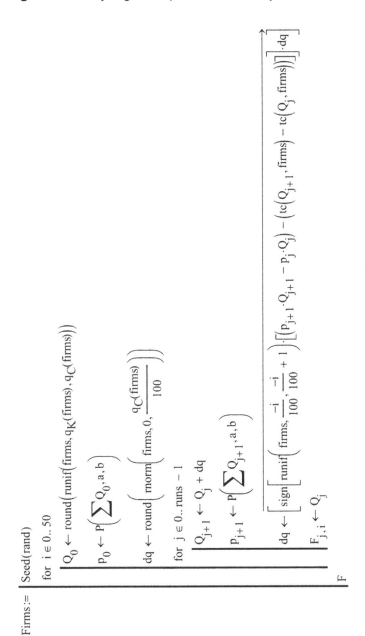

Figure 18 shows the aggregate outcome for a 100 firm industry. With no irrationality, the industry produces the amount predicted by the Keen formula. Output then increases almost monotonically as the degree of irrationality rises – until, when 20 per cent of firms are behaving irrationally at each iteration, market output converges to near the neoclassical output level.

For a degree of irrationality between 20% and 45%, the neoclassical outcome continues to dominate the simulation results. Then as irrationality rises above this level, the market effectively follows a random walk – where, curiously, profits in general tend to be *higher* than what would apply if each firm equated marginal revenue and marginal cost.

Figure 18: Market output as a function of the degree of irrationality

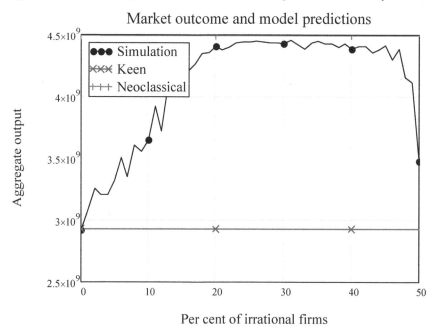

Figure 19: Sample outputs at 20% irrationality

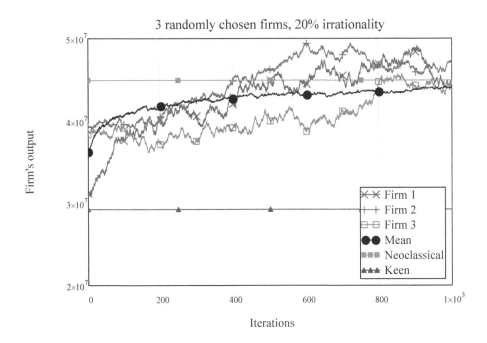

Figure 19 shows the behavior of three randomly chosen firms, and the average behavior, at a 20% level of irrationality – i.e., when one firm in five reverses any strategy that benefited it on the previous iteration.

Figure 20 shows the impact that a degree of irrationality of 20% has on firms" profits. Profit falls throughout the run, until by the end, it is almost (but not quite) as low as that caused by equating marginal revenue and marginal cost.

Figure 20: Impact of 20% irrationality on firms' profits

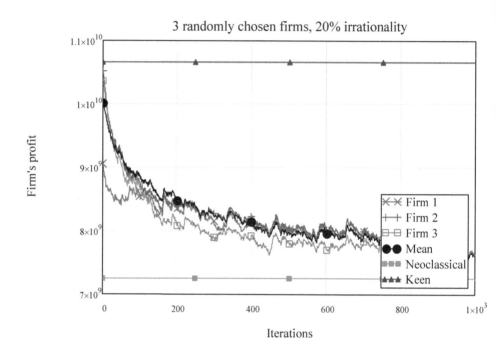

Ironically, higher profits apply if firms simply follow a random walk than if they apply the neoclassical formula (see Figure 21).

Figure 21: Firm profits with 50% irrationality

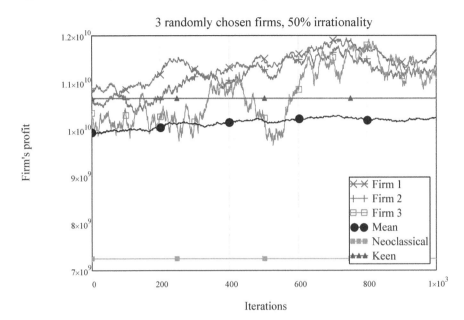

A degree of irrational behavior thus saves the neoclassical preferred outcome of price equal to marginal cost – though with some collateral damage, since it is now clearly neither profit-maximizing, nor rational. The question remains, what might help ensure this level of irrationality? Cournot-Nash game theory appears to provide an answer in strategic interactions between firms – though this answer is only unequivocal at a very superficial level of analysis.

Strategic interaction and competition

Unlike the strictly false Marshallian model of competition, Cournot-Nash game theory provides a prima facie sound basis for "perfect competition" as the outcome of strategic interactions between competitors. In Cournot-Nash game theoretic analysis, firms decide their own actions on the basis of the expected reactions of other firms, in such a way that each firm's best response is to set $MR(q_i) = MC(q_i)$. This is profit-maximizing for the firm, *in the context of the expected response of competitors to its actions*, though it results in a lower level of profit than if firms "collude" to share the monopoly level of output between them.

Up to this point, our contribution has been to show that what neoclassicals call "collusive behavior" can actually result from firms *not* reacting strategically to what other firms do – in the notation of the early part of this paper, when firms set

$$\frac{\partial q_i}{\partial q_j} = 0 \ \forall i \neq j$$

This paradox – that what neoclassical theory labels "collusion" actually occurs when firms do not react to each other – inspired us to attempt to integrate (corrected) Marshallian and Cournot-Nash theory, by making the level of strategic interaction between firms a variable. Defining the response of the ith firm to an output change by the jth firm as

$$\theta_{i,j} = \frac{\partial q_i}{\partial q_j}$$,

we then had to rework the expression for profit into one that depended entirely upon the level of strategic interaction.[15] The result of this research was a second original contribution, a generalized formula for profits in terms of the level of strategic interaction – and the discovery that the optimal level of interaction, in the context of identical firms, was zero. The derivations involved are quite complex, and they are reproduced below in their entirety.

We start from the same position as equation (1.8). For profit-maximization, we require the zero of

$$\frac{d}{dQ} \pi(q_i)$$

Debunking the theory of the firm – a chronology

We then expand this as per equation (1.9), but rather than then setting

$$\frac{d}{dQ}q_j = 1 \; \forall j$$

we work out what $\frac{d}{dQ}q_j$ is in terms of the strategic reaction coefficient $\theta_{i,j}$:

$$\frac{d}{dQ}q_i = \sum_{j=1}^{n} \frac{\partial}{\partial q_j}q_i$$

$$= \sum_{j=1}^{n} \theta_{i,j} \tag{1.14}$$

As a result, our next equation differs from equation (1.10):

$$\frac{d}{dQ}\pi(q_i) = \sum_{j=1}^{n}\left(\frac{\partial}{\partial q_j}\left(P(Q)\cdot q_i - TC(q_i)\right)\cdot\frac{d}{dQ}q_j\right)$$

$$= \sum_{j=1}^{n}\left(\frac{\partial}{\partial q_j}\left(P(Q)\cdot q_i\right)\cdot\frac{d}{dQ}q_j\right) - \sum_{j=1}^{n}\left(\frac{\partial}{\partial q_j}TC(q_i)\cdot\frac{d}{dQ}q_j\right) \tag{1.15}$$

Working firstly with the total cost component,

$$\frac{\partial}{\partial q_j}TC(q_i) = 0 \; \forall i \neq j \qquad \text{and} \qquad \frac{\partial}{\partial q_j}TC(q_i) = MC(q_i) \; \forall i = j$$

Developing an economics for the post-crisis world

Thus the cost component of the profit formula reduces to:

$$\sum_{j=1}^{n}\left(\frac{\partial}{\partial q_j}TC(q_i)\cdot\frac{d}{dQ}q_j\right)=MC(q_i)\cdot\frac{d}{dQ}q_i$$

$$=MC(q_i)\cdot\sum_{j=1}^{n}\theta_{i,j}$$

(1.16)

The revenue component involves some more intricate steps:

$$\sum_{j=1}^{n}\left(\frac{\partial}{\partial q_j}(P(Q)\cdot q_i)\cdot\frac{d}{dQ}q_j\right)$$

$$=\sum_{j=1}^{n}\left(P(Q)\cdot\frac{\partial}{\partial q_j}(q_i)\cdot\frac{d}{dQ}q_j\right)+\sum_{j=1}^{n}\left(q_i\cdot\frac{\partial}{\partial q_j}(P(Q))\cdot\frac{d}{dQ}q_j\right)$$

(1.17)

$\frac{\partial}{\partial q_j}(P(Q))$ reduces to $\frac{d}{dQ}(P(Q))$ as before, though the logic is slightly more complicated:

$$\frac{\partial}{\partial q_j}(P(Q))=\frac{\partial}{\partial Q}(P(Q))\cdot\frac{\partial}{\partial q_j}Q$$

$$=\frac{\partial}{\partial Q}(P(Q))\cdot 1$$

$$=\frac{d}{dQ}P(Q)$$

(1.18)

Making this substitution into (1.17), and using P rather than P(Q) for the sake of clarity, yields:

$$\sum_{j=1}^{n}\left(P\cdot\frac{\partial}{\partial q_j}(q_i)\cdot\frac{d}{dQ}q_j\right)+\sum_{j=1}^{n}\left(q_i\cdot\frac{dP}{dQ}\cdot\frac{d}{dQ}q_j\right)$$

$$=P\cdot\sum_{j=1}^{n}\left(\theta_{i,j}\cdot\frac{d}{dQ}q_j\right)+q_i\cdot\frac{dP}{dQ}\cdot\sum_{j=1}^{n}\left(\frac{d}{dQ}q_j\right)$$

(1.19)

Care has to be taken with expanding the expression

$$\frac{d}{dQ}q_j$$

In (1.19), since

$$\frac{d}{dQ}q_j=\sum_{j=1}^{n}\theta_{j,i}$$

but the *i* suffix here is just a placeholder for iterating over the *n* firms in the industry. We therefore make the substitution of *k* for *i* in this subscript so that we define:

$$\frac{d}{dQ}q_j=\sum_{k=1}^{n}\frac{\partial}{\partial q_k}q_j=\sum_{k=1}^{n}\theta_{j,k}$$

$$P\cdot\sum_{j=1}^{n}\left(\theta_{i,j}\cdot\frac{d}{dQ}q_j\right)+q_i\cdot\frac{dP}{dQ}\cdot\sum_{j=1}^{n}\left(\frac{d}{dQ}q_j\right)$$

$$=P\cdot\sum_{j=1}^{n}\left(\theta_{i,j}\cdot\sum_{k=1}^{n}\theta_{j,k}\right)+q_i\cdot\frac{dP}{dQ}\cdot\sum_{j=1}^{n}\left(\sum_{k=1}^{n}\theta_{j,k}\right)$$

(1.20)

Equation (1.15) finally reduces to:

$$\frac{d}{dQ}\pi(q_i) = P \cdot \sum_{j=1}^{n}\left(\sum_{k=1}^{n}\theta_{i,j}\cdot\theta_{j,k}\right) + q_i \cdot \frac{dP}{dQ}\cdot\sum_{j=1}^{n}\left(\sum_{k=1}^{n}\theta_{j,k}\right) - MC(q_i)\cdot\sum_{j=1}^{n}\theta_{i,j}$$

$$(1.21)$$

The zero of this equation determines the profit maximum for any given level of strategic interaction between firms. We can now rephrase the corrected Marshallian and the Cournot-Nash profit maxima in terms of their "conjectural variation" levels.

The Marshallian substitution is rather easy.

Given $\frac{\partial q_i}{\partial q_j} = 0 \ \forall i \neq j$ and $\frac{\partial q_i}{\partial q_j} = 1 \ \forall i = j$,

$$\sum_{j=1}^{n}\theta_{i,j} = 1 \quad \sum_{j=1}^{n}\left(\sum_{k=1}^{n}\theta_{j,k}\right)$$

; is the trace of an identity matrix so that

$$\sum_{j=1}^{n}\left(\sum_{k=1}^{n}\theta_{j,k}\right) = n$$

; and $\theta_{i,j}\cdot\theta_{j,k} = 1 \ \forall \ i = j = k$

and zero otherwise, so that

$$\sum_{j=1}^{n}\left(\sum_{k=1}^{n}\theta_{i,j}\cdot\theta_{j,k}\right) = 1$$

.

Therefore in the case of atomism, the maximum of (1.21) reduces to

$$\frac{d}{dQ}\pi(q_i) = P + q_i \cdot \frac{dP}{dQ}\cdot n - MC(q_i) = 0$$

$$(1.22)$$

This reproduces the formula derived in equation (1.13).

For the Cournot case, we start from the general situation where:

$\theta_{i,j} = \theta \ \forall \ i \neq j \ $ and $\theta_{i,i} = 1.$[16]

Then

$$\sum_{j=1}^{n} \theta_{i,j} = 1 + \sum_{i \neq j}^{n} \theta = 1 + (n-1) \cdot \theta \quad \sum_{j=1}^{n} \left(\sum_{k=1}^{n} \theta_{j,k} \right)$$

is the sum of a matrix with 1 on the diagonals and θ on the off-diagonal elements, so that

$$\sum_{j=1}^{n} \left(\sum_{k=1}^{n} \theta_{j,k} \right) = n + (n^2 - n) \cdot \theta = n\big(1 + (n-1) \cdot \theta\big)$$

$$\sum_{j=1}^{n} \left(\sum_{k=1}^{n} \theta_{i,j} \cdot \theta_{j,k} \right)$$

is the sum of each column of the matrix – which is $(n-1) \cdot \theta + 1$ – multiplied by each element of one of its columns, so that we have $(n-1) \cdot \theta + 1$ copies of $(n-1) \cdot \theta + 1$. Thus:

$$\sum_{j=1}^{n} \left(\sum_{k=1}^{n} \theta_{i,j} \cdot \theta_{j,k} \right) = \big((n-1) \cdot \theta + 1\big)^2$$

---

[16] The alleged neoclassical equilibrium occurs where $P = MC_i(q_i)$; for long-run equilibrium, only the most efficient scale of output applies so that marginal cost is identical for all firms, therefore all firms must produce at the same level of output $q_i = q = Q \div n$. For this to be stable, all firms must have the same level of strategic interaction with each other, $\theta_i = \theta$.

Developing an economics for the post-crisis world

Making these preliminary substitutions and factoring the common element $(1 + (n-1) \cdot \theta),$[17] we derive:

$$\frac{d}{dQ}\pi(q_i) = \left(1+(n-1)\cdot\theta\right)\cdot\left[P\cdot\left(1+(n-1)\cdot\theta\right)+q_i\cdot\frac{dP}{dQ}\cdot(n)-MC(q_i)\right]$$

(1.23)

Given that the Cournot-Nash "best response" results in each firm setting conventionally defined marginal revenue

$$P+q_i\cdot\frac{dP}{dQ}$$

equal to marginal cost, we can now work out the corresponding value for θ.

This is

$$\theta = \frac{1}{n\cdot E}$$

where n is the number of firms in the industry and E the market elasticity of demand

$$E = -\frac{P}{Q}\frac{dQ}{dP}$$

It is now also possible to work out the optimum value for θ, from the view of a profit-maximizing individual firm: what level of strategic response *should* a firm have to its rivals, given that its objective is to maximize its profit?

---

[17] Since θ lies in the range $[0, 1/n\cdot E]$, $\left(1+(n-1)\cdot\theta\right)\neq 0$; it can therefore be factored out.

In this generalized case of identical firms, the answer is obvious: *the optimal value of θ is zero.* As shown by equation (1.22), the profit maximum is where:

$$\frac{d}{dQ}\pi\left(q_i\right) = P + q_i \cdot \frac{dP}{dQ} \cdot n - MC\left(q_i\right) = 0$$

.

Given equation (1.23), this is only possible for $\theta = 0$. Cournot-Nash game theory is thus "A curious game. The only winning strategy is not to play"[18]. It is therefore, on closer examination, a very poor defense of the concept of perfect competition.[19]

This interpretation is given additional weight by the observation that, though the standard "Prisoners" Dilemma" presentation implies that the Cournot strategy is stable and the Keen strategy is unstable (both in a Nash equilibrium sense), the Cournot strategy is locally unstable, while the Keen strategy is locally stable.

Local stability and instability

In the Cournot-Nash game-theoretic analysis of duopoly, if firms "cooperate" and split the monopoly-level output, they make equally high profits. However, each firm has an incentive to "defect" and produce a larger amount where its marginal revenue equals its marginal cost, because it will make a higher profit still – if the other firm continues to produce its share according to the monopoly formula. This gives both firms an incentive to defect, resulting in both producing where marginal revenue equals marginal cost. This results in a lower profit for each firm than when they split the monopoly output between them, but it is a globally stable strategy, whereas all other strategy combinations are unstable.

---

[18] For those who do not know, this is a line from the 1980s movie *War Games*.
[19] It may be thought that this result is an artifact of an accidental aggregation effect from using the same reaction coefficient for all firms; we refute this by generalizing the analysis to allow for each firm to have a different reaction coefficient to the market. This research will be published in a subsequent paper.

As a result, output is higher and price lower under duopoly than monopoly, and the limit of this process as the number of firms increases is "perfect competition". This is illustrated with the example of a duopoly facing a linear market demand curve

$$P(Q) = a - b \cdot Q$$
,

with identical quadratic total cost functions

$$tc(q) = k + c \cdot q + \frac{1}{2} d \cdot q^2$$
.

Figure 22 (overleaf) shows the output combinations produced by two firms producing at either the Cournot or Keen predicted level, in terms of the demand and cost arguments.

Debunking the theory of the firm – a chronology

Figure 22: Output levels (symbolic) under Cournot & Keen strategy combinations

"Quantity Matrix" "Firms"		"Firm 1" "Cournot"		"Firm 1" "Keen"	
"Firms" "Strategy Mix"	"Firm"		"Firm"		
"Firm 2" "Cournot"	1	$\dfrac{a-c}{3\cdot b+2\cdot d}$	1	$\dfrac{a\cdot b+2\cdot a\cdot d-b\cdot c-2\cdot c\cdot d}{5\cdot b^2+10\cdot b\cdot d+4\cdot d^2}$	
"Firm 2" "Cournot"	2	$\dfrac{a-c}{3\cdot b+2\cdot d}$	2	$\dfrac{2\cdot a\cdot b+2\cdot a\cdot d-2\cdot b\cdot c-2\cdot c\cdot d}{5\cdot b^2+10\cdot b\cdot d+4\cdot d^2}$	
"Firm 2" "Keen"	1	$\dfrac{2\cdot a\cdot b+2\cdot a\cdot d-2\cdot b\cdot c-2\cdot c\cdot d}{5\cdot b^2+10\cdot b\cdot d+4\cdot d^2}$	1	$\dfrac{a-c}{4\cdot b+2\cdot d}$	
"Firm 2" "Keen"	2	$\dfrac{a\cdot b+2\cdot a\cdot d-b\cdot c-2\cdot c\cdot d}{5\cdot b^2+10\cdot b\cdot d+4\cdot d^2}$	2	$\dfrac{a-c}{4\cdot b+2\cdot d}$	

63

Developing an economics for the post-crisis world

Figure 23 shows the numeric outcomes with parameter values of a=800, $b=10^{-7}$, c=100 & $d=10^{-8}$. Clearly, the Keen/Keen combination results in the lowest aggregate output, and the highest price; Cournot/Cournot gives the highest aggregate output and lowest price; while the mixed strategy results in the highest output for one firm and the lowest for the other, with an intermediate aggregate output.

Figure 23: Output levels (numeric) under Cournot & Keen strategy combinations

"Quantity Matrix"	"Firms"	""	"Firm 1"	""	"Firm 1"
"Firms"	"Strategy Mix"	"Firm"	"Cournot"	"Firm"	"Keen"
"Firm 2"	"Cournot"	1	2.2×10^9	1	1.4×10^9
"Firm 2"	"Cournot"	2	2.2×10^9	2	2.5×10^9
"Firm 2"	"Keen"	1	2.5×10^9	1	1.7×10^9
"Firm 2"	"Keen"	2	1.4×10^9	2	1.7×10^9

Figure 24 shows why firms are tempted to "defect"—or in our terms, to move from not interacting to behaving strategically at this level of analysis. The firm that reacts to its competitor and prices where marginal revenue equals marginal cost will produce a greater quantity, which is only partly offset by a lower market price – so long as its competitor does not change its strategy. It unambiguously increases its profit, while that of its competitor falls. However, the same temptation also applies to the competitor, so both are likely to switch to interacting strategically. This is the temptation that makes the Cournot/Cournot combination a Nash Equilibrium, even though it involves an unambiguously lower profit for both firms.

Figure 24: Change in profit (symbolic) from Keen/Keen combination

"Profit Matrix" "Firms"	"Firms" "Strategy Mix"	"Profit change" "Firm"	"Firm 1" "Cournot"	"Profit Change" "Firm"	"Firm 1" "Keen"
"Firm 2"	"Cournot"	1	$\dfrac{b^2\cdot(a-c)^2}{4\cdot(2\cdot b+d)\cdot(3\cdot b+2\cdot d)^2}$	1	$\dfrac{b^2\cdot(a-c)^2\cdot\left(9\cdot b^2+20\cdot b\cdot d+8\cdot d^2\right)^2}{4\cdot(2\cdot b+d)\cdot\left(5\cdot b^2+10\cdot b\cdot d+4\cdot d^2\right)^2}$
"Firm 2"	"Cournot"	2	$\dfrac{b^2\cdot(a-c)^2}{4\cdot(2\cdot b+d)\cdot(3\cdot b+2\cdot d)^2}$	2	$\dfrac{b^2\cdot(a-c)^2\cdot\left(\dfrac{7\cdot b^2}{4}+3\cdot b\cdot d+d^2\right)}{(2\cdot b+d)\cdot\left(5\cdot b^2+10\cdot b\cdot d+4\cdot d^2\right)^2}$
"Firm 2"	"Keen"	1	$\dfrac{b^2\cdot(a-c)^2\cdot\left(\dfrac{7\cdot b^2}{4}+3\cdot b\cdot d+d^2\right)}{(2\cdot b+d)\cdot\left(5\cdot b^2+10\cdot b\cdot d+4\cdot d^2\right)^2}$	1	0
"Firm 2"	"Keen"	2	$\dfrac{b^2\cdot(a-c)^2\cdot\left(9\cdot b^2+20\cdot b\cdot d+8\cdot d^2\right)^2}{4\cdot(2\cdot b+d)\cdot\left(5\cdot b^2+10\cdot b\cdot d+4\cdot d^2\right)^2}$	2	0

Developing an economics for the post-crisis world

Figure 25 shows the numeric consequence, given the example parameters used.

Figure 25: Change in profit (numeric) from Keen/Keen combination

"Profit Matrix"	"Firms"	"Profit change"	"Firm 1"	"Profit Change"	"Firm 1"
"Firms"	"Strategy Mix"	"Firm"	"Cournot"	"Firm"	"Keen"
"Firm 2"	"Cournot"	1	-5.7×10^{10}	1	-1.8×10^{11}
"Firm 2"	"Cournot"	2	-5.7×10^{10}	2	1.3×10^{11}
"Firm 2"	"Keen"	1	1.3×10^{11}	1	0
"Firm 2"	"Keen"	2	-1.8×10^{11}	2	0

So far, the argument looks conclusive for the Cournot-Nash Equilibrium as the outcome of strategic interaction, and competition thus works to cause higher aggregate output and lower prices than would apply with fewer firms in the industry. Add more firms, and ultimately you converge to where price equals marginal cost – the Holy Grail of perfect competition.

The acknowledged wrinkle in this argument is that, with infinitely repeated games, the Nash equilibrium is the Keen strategy – called "collusion" or "cooperate" in the literature because, before our critique, it was believed that the only way firms could work this amount out was by acting as a cartel.[20] It's possible to "rescue" perfect competition by assuming finitely repeated games, showing that "defect" (or Keen) dominates the final play, reverse-iterating back to the second last, and by finite backwards regression arrive at "defect" as the ideal strategy for all iterations. But this is obviously weak as an analogy to actual competition, where the infinitely repeated game is closer to the reality of an indefinite future of competition – even if some competitors do exit an industry, their rivals can never know when this might happen.

---

[20] Of course, neoclassical economists still believe this today, and will doubtless continue believing it, given how dogma has almost always overruled logic in the development of economic theory.

Most game theorists express puzzlement with this dilemma: a strategy is dominant in a one shot, but not in a repeated game. So "collusion" (or more correctly, "non-interaction") appears dominant, and it appears that firms will tend not to compete over time.[21]

There is an additional wrinkle that possibly explains this known dilemma (and the simulation results shown in Figure 15):[22] while the Cournot strategy is a Nash Equilibrium, it is locally unstable, and while the Keen strategy is not a Nash Equilibrium, it is locally stable. This occurs not because of collusion, but because strategic interactions – which we might describe as a "Meta-Nash Dynamic" – lead from the Cournot equilibrium to the Keen.

One firm may benefit from a strategic change – say, Firm 1 increasing its output from that in the Keen/Keen output pair, while Firm 2 reduces it. The strategy pair would then be "increase, decrease" (or "+1/-1") and the profit outcomes "increase, decrease". In an iterative search for the profit-maximizing level, this would encourage Firm 1 to continue increasing its output, which would take it in the direction of the Cournot equilibrium. However Firm 2, having lost from that strategic combination, will change its strategy – and rather than decreasing its output further, it will increase its output. Then the strategy pair will be "increase, increase" and the profit outcomes are "decrease, decrease". As a result, both firms will change their strategy to "decrease", and head back to the Keen equilibrium.

---

[21] We suspect that this dilemma explains the paradox that neoclassical economists, who are normally so opposed to government intervention, support "competition policy", which in effect forces firms to compete with each other.

[22] One curious feature of this simulation is that the convergence result is dependent, not on the number of firms – as neoclassical theory falsely asserts – but on the dispersal of output changes by each firm. The higher the size, relative to output, of the randomly allocated output changes, the higher the likelihood that the end result will be convergence to the Cournot equilibrium rather than the Keen. This result is reported in Keen & Standish 2006.

Figure 26: Profit changes for Firm 1 and Firm 2 from output changes from Keen equilibrium

$$
\begin{pmatrix}
\text{"Firm 1"} & \text{"-1"} & \text{"0"} & \text{"+1"} \\
\text{"-1"} & -2.1\times10^{-7} & -166.7 & -333.3 \\
\text{"0"} & 166.7 & 0 & -166.7 \\
\text{"+1"} & 333.3 & 166.7 & -2.1\times10^{-7} \\
\text{"Firm 2"} & \text{"-1"} & \text{"0"} & \text{"+1"} \\
\text{"-1"} & -2.1\times10^{-7} & 166.7 & 333.3 \\
\text{"0"} & -166.7 & 0 & 166.7 \\
\text{"+1"} & -333.3 & -166.7 & -2.1\times10^{-7}
\end{pmatrix}
$$

Figure 26 illustrates this using the example parameters above.[23] The top half shows the outcome for Firm 1; the bottom half, for Firm 2; strategy settings by Firm 1 are shown by column 1, and settings by Firm 2 by row one. A strategy pair of "+1/-1" results in Firm 1 increasing profit by 333, which clearly encourages Firm 1 to continue increasing production. However, that combination causes a drop in profits of 333 for Firm 2, which will cause Firm 2 to swap strategies – say from "-1" to "+1". That will then switch the market situation to the "+1/+1" combination, where both firms suffer a fall in profits (and the fall in profits gets larger for larger output increases). Both firms are then likely to switch to reducing output. The Keen equilibrium is thus locally stable because of strategic interactions.

The Cournot equilibrium, on the other hand, is locally unstable. Figure 27 shows the outcomes for changes of one unit for each firm. The strategy pair "+1/-1" results in increase in profits for Firm 1 and a fall in profits for Firm 2, as it did in the Keen equilibrium. Firm 1 will then be encouraged to continue increasing production, while Firm 2 will be encouraged to switch from reducing output to increasing output. The next strategy pair is thus likely to

---

[23] The outcome applies so long as a>c, b<a and d<c; all these are fundamental conditions for a market to exist in the first instance. a<c, for example, would set the equilibrium market output at less than zero.

be "+1/+1" (or some higher combination). This also causes a loss for both firms, so another switch in strategy is likely – to reducing output.

Figure 27: Profit changes for Firm 1 and Firm 2 from output changes from Cournot equilibrium

$$
\begin{pmatrix}
\text{"Firm 1"} & \text{"-1"} & \text{"0"} & \text{"+1"} \\
\text{"-1"} & 218.7 & -1.1 \times 10^{-7} & -218.8 \\
\text{"0"} & 218.7 & 0 & -218.7 \\
\text{"+1"} & 218.7 & -1.1 \times 10^{-7} & -218.8 \\
\text{"Firm 2"} & \text{"-1"} & \text{"0"} & \text{"+1"} \\
\text{"-1"} & 218.7 & 218.7 & 218.7 \\
\text{"0"} & -1.1 \times 10^{-7} & 0 & -1.1 \times 10^{-7} \\
\text{"+1"} & -218.8 & -218.7 & -218.8
\end{pmatrix}
$$

Unlike the Keen/Keen situation, the strategy pair "-1/-1" from the Cournot equilibrium results in an increase in profits for *both* firms – and larger reductions in output cause larger increases in profit. Further movement away from the Cournot equilibrium is rewarded, so that both firms are likely to adopt the strategy of reducing output, until they reach the Keen equilibrium – with absolutely no "collusion" taking place. The Cournot equilibrium is thus locally unstable, not because of collusion, but because of strategic interactions.

Figure 28 and Figure 29 put the impact of strategic interactions graphically: in each case the predicted output pair (Keen/Keen and Cournot/Cournot respectively) is in the middle of the box. While firms are not behaving collusively, the only strategy pairs that have a chance to be self-sustaining are those that have a positive impact on the profit of both parties – since as explained above, any strategy that has a negative impact will necessarily mean a change in behavior by one or both firms. Therefore, the shape of the aggregate profit "hill" indicates whether any sustaining strategic interactions exist.

Developing an economics for the post-crisis world

Figure 28 confirms that there are no such interactions in the vicinity of the Keen equilibrium: all strategic pairs involve a fall in aggregate profits relative to the starting point. The Keen equilibrium is thus locally stable.

Figure 28: Impact of strategic interactions on profit near Keen equilibrium

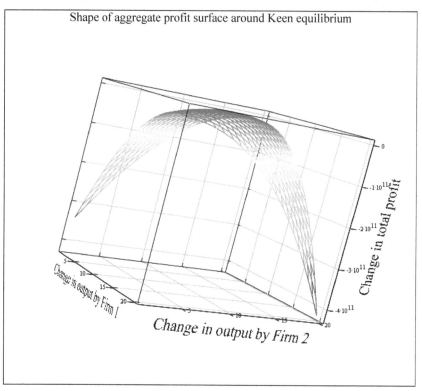

M

The Cournot equilibrium, on the other hand, is locally unstable, because aggregate profit will rise if both firms reduce output (see Figure 29).

70

Figure 29: Impact of strategic interactions on profit near Cournot equilibrium

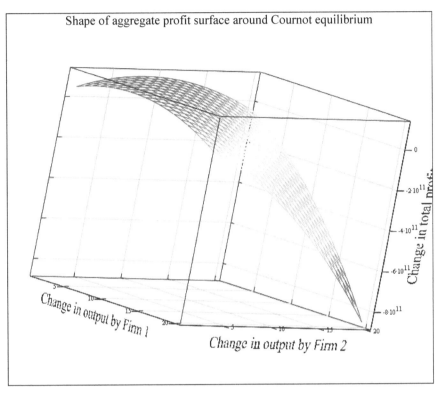

Shape of aggregate profit surface around Cournot equilibrium

N

Thus, though the Cournot-Nash defense of perfect competition is not strictly false, in practice it is fragile. It appears that, if a profit-maximizing level of output per firm can be identified, then rational profit-maximizing firms will identify it, regardless of how many of them there are in an industry.[24] The Holy Grail of "perfect competition", though theoretically attainable via strategic interaction, is a will o' the wisp.

So too, ironically, is the argument that there is a profit-maximizing level of output per firm.

---

[24] Subject to the one caveat mentioned in Footnote 22.

The empirical reality of competition

A plethora of empirical studies have established that at least 89 per cent of output – and perhaps as much as 95 per cent – is produced under conditions of constant or falling marginal cost, and rising economies of scale.[25] Given such circumstances, there is no profit-maximizing level of output for the individual firm: so long as the sale price exceeds average costs, the firm will profit from additional sales. The key presumption of the neoclassical model – that there is a profit-maximizing level of sales – is thus not fulfilled in the real world.

The most recent such survey was carried out by Alan Blinder and a team of PhD students in 1998. Blinder's results are also arguably the most authoritative, given the scale of his study, and Blinder's prestige as an economist.

Blinder et al. surveyed a representative weighted sample of US non-agricultural corporations with annual sales of more than US$10 million; a 61% response rate resulted in a study of 200 corporations whose combined output represented 7.6% of the USA's GDP. The interviews were face to face, with Blinder and a team of Economics PhD students conducting the interviews; the interviewees were top executives of the firms, with 25% being the President or CEO, and 45% a Vice President.

Blinder summarized the results in the following way:

> "First, about 85 percent of all the goods and services in the U.S. nonfarm business sector are sold to 'regular customers' with whom sellers have an ongoing relationship … And about 70 percent of sales are business to business rather than from businesses to consumers…
>
> Second, and related, contractual rigidities … are extremely common … about one-quarter of output is sold under contracts that fix nominal prices for a nontrivial period of

---

[25] See Lee 1998 for a comprehensive survey of the 20th century studies.

time. And it appears that discounts from contract prices are rare. Roughly another 60 percent of output is covered by Okun-style implicit contracts which slow down price adjustments.

Third, firms typically report fixed costs that are quite high relative to variable costs. And they rarely report the upward-sloping marginal cost curves that are ubiquitous in economic theory. Indeed, downward-sloping marginal cost curves are more common... If these answers are to be believed ... then [a good deal of microeconomic theory] is called into question... For example, price cannot approximate marginal cost in a competitive market if fixed costs are very high" (p. 302).

The key final point about falling marginal cost deserves elaboration. Given that, as they discovered, "marginal cost is not a natural mental construct for most executives." they translated marginal cost into "variable costs of producing additional units," and posed the following question:

"B7(a). Some companies find that their variable costs per unit are roughly constant when production rises. Others incur either higher or lower variable costs of producing additional units when they raise production.

How would you characterize the behavior of your own variable costs of producing additional units as production rises?" (Blinder 1998: 102.)

The survey team collated the responses into five groups, as summarized in Table 4:

Table 4: Marginal cost structure of American corporations (Blinder et al. 1998: 102-103)

Structure of Marginal Costs	Percentage of firms
Decreasing	32.6
Decreasing with discrete jumps	7.9
Constant	40
Constant with discrete jumps	7.9
Increasing	11.1

Blinder et al. pithily observed that:

> "The overwhelmingly bad news here (for economic theory) is that, apparently, only 11 percent of GDP is produced under conditions of rising marginal cost" (p. 102).

The overall results of Blinder's survey are summarized in Table 2. Given the empirically common circumstances detailed here, the pre-requisites for being able to identify a profit-maximizing level of output do not exist for at least 89 per cent of US firms.[26] Instead, for these firms, the only profit-maximizing strategy is to sell as much as they can – and at the expense, where possible, of competitors" sales.

---

[26] We say at least because all previous surveys have reported a lower proportion of products that are produced under conditions of diminishing marginal productivity – typically 5 per cent of output (Eiteman & Guthrie 1952).

Table 5: Summary of Blinder et al.'s empirical findings

Summary of Selected Factual Results Price Policy	
Median number of price changes in a year	1.4
Mean lag before adjusting price months following:	
Demand Increase	2.9
Demand Decrease	2.9
Cost Increase	2.8
Cost Decrease	3.3
Percent of firms which:	
Report annual price reviews	45
Change prices all at once	74
Change prices in small steps	16
Have nontrivial costs of adjusting prices	43
of which related primarily to:	
the frequency of price changes	69
the size of price changes	14
Sales	
Estimated percent of GDP sold under contracts which fix prices	28
Percent of firms which report implicit contracts	65
Percent of sales which are made to:	
Consumers	21
Businesses	70
Other (principally government)	9
Regular customers	85
Percent of firms whose sales are:	
Relatively sensitive to the state of the economy	43
Relatively Insensitive to the state of the economy	39
Costs	
Percent of firms which can estimate costs at least moderately well	87
Mean percentage of costs which are fixed	44
Percentage of firms for which marginal costs are:	
Increasing	11
Constant	48
Decreasing	41

The only practical way that this can be done is via product differentiation, and that indeed is the obvious form that real competition actually takes. Innovation and heterogeneity are the true hallmarks of competition, yet these concepts are effectively excluded by the neoclassical model.

A model of how this actual form of competition works would be extremely useful to economic theory – and perhaps even to economic policy, if we could scientifically identify those industry structures that truly promote innovation. The continued teaching of the neoclassical model, and the continued development of a research tradition in which rising marginal cost plays a key role, are a hindrance to developing an adequate model of real world competition.

Our closing observation on this theory is perhaps the most important. A theory is more than a scholastic exercise: a good theory is also an attempt to understand reality, and, where possible, to alter it for the better. There are, therefore, few things more dangerous than an applied bad theory. Unfortunately, neoclassical competition theory is applied throughout the world, in the guise of policies intended to promote competition.

The anti-capitalist nature of neoclassical competition policy

The neoclassical vision of competition has been enshrined in competition policies adopted by governments and applied to key industries such as telecommunications, power, sanitation, and water supply. The major practical implications of accepted theory are that more firms equates to increased competition, increased competition means higher output at lower prices, and market price should ideally be equal to marginal cost.

Since the theory is flawed, these implications are at best unproven, and at worst false. There are now numerous instances around the world where competition policies have resulted in deleterious outcomes; a special issue of *Utilities Policy* in 2004 details several of these for the USA (and Australia). Loube, for example, examined the US Telecom Act of 1996, and found that "this policy has actually raised prices for residential customers" (Trebing & Miller 2004: 106).

Proponents of competition policy normally ascribe such outcomes to poor implementation of policy, poor regulatory oversight, or unanticipated circumstances. However, if the theory is flawed as we argue, then these outcomes are not accidents, but the systemic results of imposing a false theory on actual markets. Some predictable negative consequences are rising costs due to reduced economies of scale, underinvestment caused by imposed prices that lie below average cost, and reduced rates of innovation in related industries, caused by the inadequate "competitive" provision of infrastructure.

That these policies were imposed in a well-meaning attempt to improve social welfare cannot detract from the fact that, if the theory guiding these policies was false, then the policies are likely to cause more harm than good. Real world markets would function far better if competition policy, as it stands, were abolished.

Conclusion

A careful examination of the neoclassical theory of competition thus finds that it has little, if any, true content.

The Marshallian argument, which forms the backbone of neoclassical pedagogy, is strictly false in its belief that a downward-sloping market demand curve is compatible with horizontal individual firm demand curves. Once this error is corrected, the model's major conclusion, that competitive industries are better than concentrated ones, is overturned. Given identical demand and cost conditions, competitive industries will produce the same output as monopolies, and sell at the same price – and there are good grounds for expecting that monopolies would have lower costs (see Appendix One).

The Cournot analysis is mathematically correct, but subject to a problem of local instability as well as the known dilemma of repeated games. If it is interpreted as an "as if" explanation for what happens between competing firms in an industry – i.e., it proposes that firms do not actually solve the mathematics to find their Nash equilibrium output levels, but instead

77

undertake an iterative search of the output-profit space – then this iterative search will lead to the Keen equilibrium, not the Cournot-Nash one, because the former is locally stable under strategic interactions, while the latter is not.

Given this intrinsic barrenness of the theory, its empirical irrelevance is even more important. Neoclassical economists have ignored a multitude of empirical papers that show that marginal cost does not rise, that firms do not compete on price, and so on, on the basis of Friedman's belief that asking businessmen what they do is not "a relevant test of the associated hypothesis." But if the "associated hypothesis" is in fact false, or irrelevant, then "asking businessmen what they do" is at least a good place from which to derive stylized facts that a relevant hypothesis would have to explain. It is high time that economists abandoned what superficially appears to be "high theory", and got their hands dirty with real empirical research into actual firms and actual competition.

Here the picture that emerges from even a cursory examination of the data is very different to neoclassical belief. Table 6 shows the aggregate distribution of firm sizes in the USA in 2002: large firms make up well under 0.3 per cent of the total number of firms, but are responsible for over 60 per cent of sales.

Table 6: US firm size data (US Office of Small Business Advocacy)

Industry		2002		
		Total	0-499	500+
Total	Firms	5,697,759	5,680,914	16,845
	Estab.	7,200,770	6,172,809	1,027,961
	Emp.	112,400,654	56,366,292	56,034,362
	Ann. pay.($000)	3,943,179,606	1,777,049,574	2,166,130,032
	Receipts($000)	22,062,528,196	8,558,731,333	13,503,796,863

At the same time, small firms are not negligible: all industries are characterized by a wide distribution of firm sizes, from sole trader through to large conglomerates (see Table 7).

Debunking the theory of the firm – a chronology

Perhaps the real story of competition is the survival of such diversity.

Table 7: Distribution of firm sizes in manufacturing (US SBA)

	Manufacturing Firms	Estab.	Emp.	Ann. pay. ($000)	Receipts ($000)
Total	297,873	344,341	14,393,609	580,356,005	3,937,164,576
0 *	21,731	21,761	0	2,231,805	15,166,970
1-4	97,197	97,232	219,951	5,823,048	27,659,982
5-9	55,597	55,702	372,245	10,533,204	44,184,220
10-19	46,851	47,200	639,036	19,888,764	80,892,263
0-19	221,376	221,895	1,231,232	38,476,821	167,903,435
20-99	58,198	62,443	2,375,691	82,257,351	346,024,892
100-499	14,124	23,727	2,488,018	91,152,085	460,526,128
0-499	293,698	308,065	6,094,941	211,886,257	974,454,455
500+	4,175	36,276	8,298,668	368,469,748	2,962,710,121

In the light of both its theoretical weaknesses and its irrelevance to the empirical data, Sraffa's advice in 1930 about what to do with Marshall's theory bear repeating today, not only in relation to Marshall's theory, but even to the Cournot-Nash approach:

> "... the theory cannot be interpreted in a way which makes it logically sell-consistent and, at the same time, reconciles it with the facts it sets out to explain. Mr. Robertson's remedy is to discard mathematics, and he suggests that my remedy is to discard the facts; perhaps I ought to have explained that, in the circumstances, I think it is Marshall's theory that should be discarded" (Sraffa 1930: 93).

The neoclassical theory of competition is a hindrance to understanding real markets and real competition, and it should be abandoned.

Appendices

Appendix One: Conditions for comparability of cost structures

Economists blithely draw diagrams like Figure 30 below to compare monopoly with perfect competition. As shown above, the basis of the comparison is false: given Marshallian assumptions, an industry with many "perfectly competitive" firms will produce the same amount as a monopoly facing identical demand and cost conditions – and both industry structures will lead to a "deadweight loss". However, in general, small competitive firms would have different cost conditions to a single firm – not only because of economies of scale spread result in lower per unit fixed costs, but also because of the impact of economies of scale on marginal costs.

Figure 30: Mankiw's monopoly versus perfect competition comparison

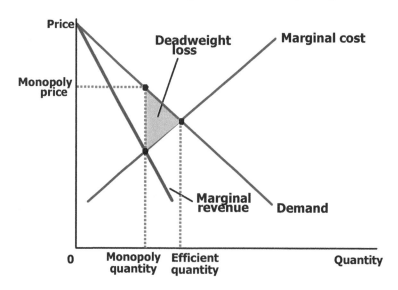

Debunking the theory of the firm – a chronology

Rosput (1993) gives a good illustration of this latter point in relation to gas utilities. One of the fixed costs of gas supply is the pipe; one of the variable costs is the compression needed to move the gas along the pipe. A larger diameter pipe allows a larger volume of gas to be passed with lower compression losses, so that the larger scale of output results in lower marginal costs:

> "Simply stated, the necessary first investment in infrastructure is the construction of the pipeline itself. Thereafter, additional units of throughput can be economically added through the use of horsepower to compress the gas up to a certain point where the losses associated with the compression make the installation of additional pipe more economical than the use of additional horsepower of compression. The loss of energy is, of course, a function of, among other things, the diameter of the pipe. Thus, at the outset, the selection of pipe diameter is a critical ingredient in determining the economics of future expansions of the installed pipe: the larger the diameter, the more efficient are the future additions of capacity and hence the lower the marginal costs of future units of output" (Rosput 1993: 288).

Thus a single large supplier is likely to have lower costs – in which case, the marginal cost curve for the monopoly should be drawn *below* that for the competitive industry. Given the same demand curve and the same profit-maximizing behavior, a monopoly is thus likely to produce a higher output than a competitive industry, and at a lower cost.

The cost examples in this paper were artificially constructed to ensure that the assumption of identical costs embodied in Figure 30 were fulfilled – something that we doubt has been done by neoclassical authors in comparable papers. The cost functions were:

$$Monopoly : MC(Q) = C + D \cdot Q + E \cdot Q^2$$
$$Competitive : mc(q,n) = C + D \cdot n \cdot q + E \cdot n^2 \cdot q^2$$
(1.24)

Obviously, it is very arbitrary to have the number of firms in an industry as an argument in the marginal cost function of a single firm – and also highly unlikely. Yet without that "heroic" assumption, the aggregate of marginal costs curves for a competitive industry will *necessarily* differ from the marginal cost curve for a monopoly. If a monopoly has greater access to economies of scale than smaller competitive firms, as in Rosput's example of gas transmission, then on conventional profit-maximizing grounds, a monopoly would produce a higher output for a lower price.

It is also easily shown that the neoclassical pedagogic assumption that the same marginal cost curve can be drawn for a competitive industry and a monopoly is true in only two circumstances: either the monopoly simply changes the ownership of plants in the industry – so that there is no technical difference between one industry structure and the other – or both industry structures face identical *constant* marginal costs.[27]

Marginal cost is the inverse of marginal product, which in turn is the derivative of total product. The condition of identical marginal costs – that is, that the marginal cost curve for a monopoly is identically equal to the sum of the marginal cost curves of an industry with many competitive firms, for all relevant levels of output – therefore requires that the total products of two different industry structures differ only by a constant. This constant can be set to zero, since output is zero with zero variable inputs.

Consider a competitive industry with n firms, each employing x workers, and a monopoly with m plants, each employing y workers, where $n>m$. Graphically this condition can be shown as in Figure 31.

---

[27] This argument was first published in Keen 2004a.

Figure 31: Production functions required for identical marginal cost curves

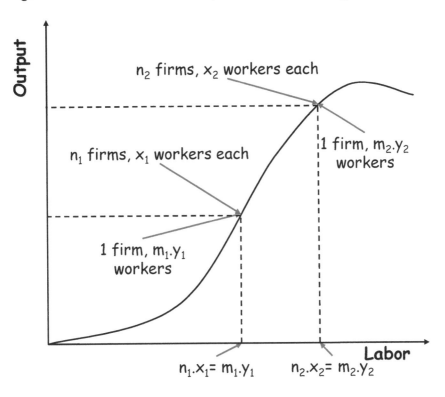

Using *f* for the production function of the competitive firms, and *g* for the production function of the monopoly, the equality of total products condition can be put in the following form:

$$n \cdot f(x) = m \cdot g(y)$$

(1.25)

Substitute $y = \dfrac{n \cdot x}{m}$ into (1) and differentiate both sides of (1.25) by *n*:

$$f(x) = \frac{x}{m} \cdot g'\left(\frac{n \cdot x}{m}\right)$$

(1.26)

This gives us a second expression for f. Equating these two definitions yields:

$$\frac{g\left(\frac{n \cdot x}{m}\right)}{n} = \frac{x}{m} \cdot g'\left(\frac{n \cdot x}{m}\right)$$

or

$$\frac{g'\left(\frac{n \cdot x}{m}\right)}{g\left(\frac{n \cdot x}{m}\right)} = \frac{m}{n \cdot x}$$

(1.27)

The substitution of $y = \frac{n \cdot x}{m}$ yields an expression involving the differential of the log of g:

$$\frac{g'(y)}{g(y)} = \frac{1}{y}$$

(1.28)

Integrating both sides yields:

$$\ln\left(g\left(y\right)\right) = \ln\left(y\right) + c$$

(1.29)

Thus g is a constant returns production function:

$$g\left(y\right) = C \cdot y$$

(1.30)

It follows that f is the *same* constant returns production function:

$$f\left(x\right) = \frac{m}{n} \cdot C \cdot \frac{n \cdot x}{m}$$

(1.31)

With both f and g being identical constant returns production functions, the marginal products and hence the marginal costs of the competitive industry and monopoly are constant and identical. The general rule, therefore, is that welfare comparisons of perfect competition and monopoly are only definitive when the competitive firms and the monopoly operate under conditions of constant identical marginal cost.

References

Blinder, A.S., Canetti, E., Lebow, D., & Rudd, J., (1998). *Asking About Prices: a New Approach to Understanding Price Stickiness*, Russell Sage Foundation, New York.

Eiteman, W.J. & Guthrie, G.E., (1952). "The shape of the average cost curve", *American Economic Review* 42: 832-838.

Craig Freedman (1998). "No ends to means: George Stigler's profit motive", *Journal of Post Keynesian Economics* 20; 621-648.

Milton Friedman (1953). "The Methodology of Positive Economics", in *Essays in Positive Economics*, University of Chicago Press, Chicago: 3-43.

Haines, W.W., (1948). "Capacity production and the least cost point", *American Economic Review* 38: 617-624.

Steve Keen (1993a). "The misinterpretation of Marx's theory of value", *Journal of the History of Economic Thought*, 15 (2), Fall, 282-300.

Steve Keen (1993b). "Use-value, exchange-value, and the demise of Marx's labor theory of value", *Journal of the History of Economic Thought*, 15 (1), Spring, 107-121.

Steve Keen (2001). *Debunking Economics*, Pluto Press & Zed Books, Sydney & London.

Steve Keen (2004a). "Why economics must abandon its theory of the firm", in Salzano, M., & Kirman, A. (eds.), *Economics: Complex Windows*, Springer, New York, pp. 65-88.

Steve Keen (2004b). "Deregulator: Judgment Day for Microeconomics", *Utilities Policy*, 12: 109–125.

Steve Keen (2004c). "Improbable, Incorrect or Impossible: The persuasive but flawed mathematics of microeconomics", in Fullbrook, E. (ed.), *Student's Guide to What's Wrong with Economics*, Routledge, London, pp. 209-222.

Steve Keen and Russell Standish (2005). "Irrationality in the neoclassical definition of rationality", *American Journal of Applied Sciences* (Sp.Issue): 61-68.

Steve Keen and Russell Standish (2006). "Profit Maximization, Industry Structure, and Competition: A critique of neoclassical theory", *Physica A* 370: 81-85.

Lee, F., (1998). *Post Keynesian Price Theory*, Cambridge University Press, Cambridge.

A. Mas-Colell, M.D. Whinston, J.R. Green (1995). *Microeconomics*, Oxford University Press, New York.

Piero Sraffa (1930). "Increasing Returns And The Representative Firm A Symposium", Economic Journal 40 pp.79-116.

George J. Stigler (1957), Perfect competition, historically contemplated. *Journal of Political Economy* 65: 1-17.

Harry M. Trebing and Edythe S. Miller (2004). "Introduction", *Utilities Policy* 12: 105-108.

Leon Walras (1899 [1954]). *Elements of Pure Economics*, 4th edition, George Allen & Unwin, London.

Economic growth, asset markets and the credit accelerator

According to the U.S. National Bureau of Economic Research, the "Great Recession" is now two years behind us, but the recovery that normally follows a recession has not occurred. While growth did rise for a while, it has been anaemic compared to the norm after a recession, and it is already trending down. Growth needs to exceed 3 per cent per annum to reduce unemployment – the rule of thumb known as Okun's Law[28] – and it needs to be substantially higher than this to make serious inroads into it. Instead, growth barely peeped its head above Okun's level. It is now below it again, and trending down. Unemployment is therefore rising once more, and with it, Obama's chances of re-election are rapidly fading.

Figure 32

USA Real GDP Growth Rate

www.debtdeflation.com/blogs

---

[28] http://en.wikipedia.org/wiki/Okun's_law

Obama was assured by his advisors that this wouldn't happen. Right from the first "Economic Report of the President"[29] that he received from Bush's outgoing Chairman of the Council of Economic Advisers Ed Lazear in January 2009[30], he was assured that "the deeper the downturn, the stronger the recovery". On the basis of the regression shown in Chart 1-9 of that report (on page 54), I am sure that Obama was told that real growth would probably exceed 5 per cent per annum – because this is what Ed Lazear told me after my session at the Australian Conference of Economists in September 2009.

Figure 33

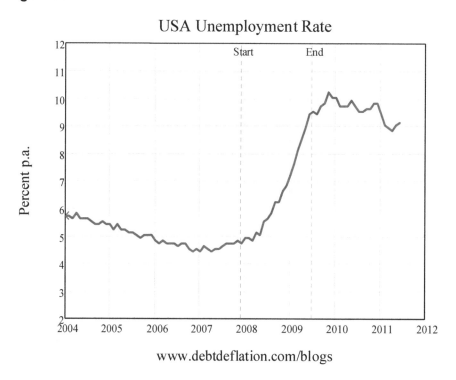

USA Unemployment Rate

www.debtdeflation.com/blogs

---

[29] http://www.gpoaccess.gov/eop/download.html
[30] http://www.gpoaccess.gov/eop/2009/2009_erp.pdf

Economic growth, asset markets and the credit accelerator

Figure 34

Chart 1-9 **Recessions and Recession Recoveries**
GDP growth over the eight quarters following a recession tends to be higher after more severe recessions.
Growth over the eight quarters subsequent to GDP trough (percent)

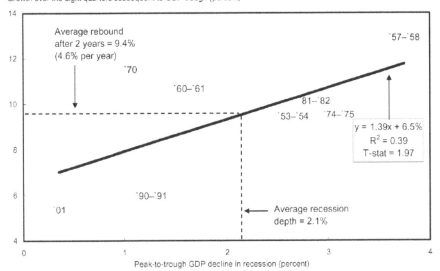

Note: Datapoint labels indicate year of recession. The depth of recession is meausured from the peak GDP quarter to the minimum GDP quarter. The recovery is the eight-quarter growth from that minimum-GDP quarter.
Source: Department of Commerce (Bureau of Economic Analysis).

I disputed this analysis then (see "In the Dark on Cause and Effect, Debtwatch, Lazear, October 2009"), and events have certainly borne out my analysis rather than the conventional wisdom. To give an idea of how wrong this guidance was, the peak to trough decline in the Great Recession – the x-axis in Lazear's Chart – was over 6 percent. His regression equation therefore predicted that GDP growth in the 2 years after the recession ended would have been over 12 percent. If this equation had born fruit, US Real GDP would be $17.6 trillion in June 2011, versus the recorded $15 trillion in March 2011.

So why has the conventional wisdom been so wrong? Largely because it has ignored the role of private debt.

Figure 35

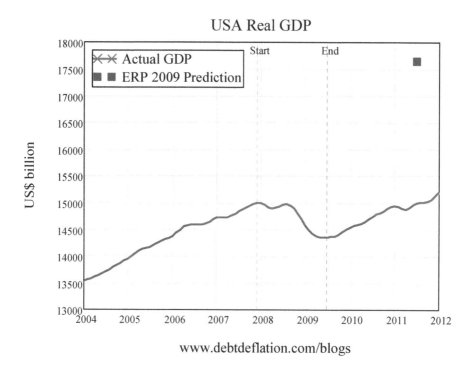

Economic growth, asset markets and the credit accelerator

Neoclassical economists ignore the level of private debt, on the basis of the *a priori* argument that "one man's liability is another man's asset", so that the aggregate level of debt has no macroeconomic impact. They reason that the increase in the debtor's spending power is offset by the fall in the lender's spending power, and there is therefore no change to aggregate demand.

Lest it be said that I'm parodying neoclassical economics, or relying on what lesser lights believe when the leaders of the profession know better, here are two apposite quotes from Ben Bernanke and Paul Krugman.

Economic growth, asset markets and the credit accelerator

Bernanke in his *Essays on the Great Depression*, explains why neoclassical economists didn't take Fisher's paper "Debt Deflation Theory of Great Depressions"[31] seriously:

> Fisher's idea was less influential in academic circles, though, because of the counterargument that debt-deflation represented no more than a redistribution from one group (debtors) to another (creditors). Absent implausibly large differences in marginal spending propensities among the groups, it was suggested, pure redistributions should have no significant macro-economic effects...[32]

Paul Krugman in his most recent draft academic paper[33] on the crisis and co-author Gauti B. Eggertsson write:

> Given both the prominence of debt in popular discussion of our current economic difficulties and the long tradition of invoking debt as a key factor in major economic contractions, one might have expected debt to be at the heart of most mainstream macroeconomic models – especially the analysis of monetary and fiscal policy. Perhaps somewhat surprisingly, however, it is quite common to abstract altogether from this feature of the economy. Even economists trying to analyze the problems of monetary and fiscal policy at the zero lower bound – and yes, that includes the authors – have often adopted representative-agent models in which everyone is alike, and in which the shock that pushes the economy into a situation in which even a zero interest rate isn't low enough takes the form of a shift in everyone's preferences...

---

[31] Fisher, Irving. 1933. "The Debt-Deflation Theory of Great Depressions." *Econometrica*, 1(4), 337-57.
[32] Bernanke, Ben S. 2000. *Essays on the Great Depression*. Princeton: Princeton University Press, p. 24.
[33] Krugman, Paul and Gauti B. Eggertsson. 2010. "Debt, Deleveraging, and the Liquidity Trap: A Fisher-Minsky-Koo Approach [2nd Draft 2/14/2011]," New York: Federal Reserve Bank of New York & Princeton University, p. 2,
http://www.princeton.edu/~pkrugman/debt_deleveraging_ge_pk.pdf

And:

> Ignoring the foreign component, or looking at the world as a whole, the overall level of debt makes no difference to aggregate net worth -- one person's liability is another person's asset.[34]

They are profoundly wrong on this point because neoclassical economists do not understand how money is created by the private banking system – despite decades of empirical research to the contrary, they continue to cling to the textbook vision of banks as mere intermediaries between savers and borrowers.

This is bizarre, since as long as 4 decades ago, the actual situation was put very simply by the then Senior Vice President, Federal Reserve Bank of New York, Alan Holmes. Holmes explained why the then faddish Monetarist policy of controlling inflation by controlling the growth of Base Money had failed, saying that it suffered from "a naive assumption" that:

> the banking system only expands loans after the [Federal Reserve] System (or market factors) have put reserves in the banking system. *In the real world, banks extend credit, creating deposits in the process, and look for the reserves later.* The question then becomes one of whether and how the Federal Reserve will accommodate the demand for reserves. In the very short run, the Federal Reserve has little or no choice about accommodating that demand; over time, its influence can obviously be felt[35] (emphasis added).

The empirical fact that "loans create deposits" means that the change in the level of private debt is matched by a change in the level of money, which boosts aggregate demand. The level of private debt therefore cannot be ignored – and the fact that neoclassical economists did ignore it (and, with

---

[34] Ibid, p. 3.
[35] Holmes, Alan R. 1969. "Operational Constraints on the Stabilization of Money Supply Growth," F. E. Morris, *Controlling Monetary Aggregates*. Nantucket Island: The Federal Reserve Bank of Boston, 65-77.

the likes of Greenspan running the Fed, actively promoted its growth) is why this is no "garden variety" downturn.

In all the post-WWII recessions on which Lazear's regression was based, the downturn ended when the growth of private debt turned positive again and boosted aggregate demand. This of itself is not a bad thing: as Schumpeter argued decades ago, in a well-functioning capitalist system, the main recipients of credit are entrepreneurs who have an idea, but not the money needed to put it into action:

> "[I]n so far as credit cannot be given out of the results of past enterprise ... it can only consist of credit means of payment created ad hoc, which can be backed neither by money in the strict sense nor by products already in existence...

> It provides us with the connection between lending and credit means of payment, and leads us to what I regard as the nature of the credit phenomenon... credit is essentially the creation of purchasing power for the purpose of transferring it to the entrepreneur, but not simply the transfer of existing purchasing power."[36]

It becomes a bad thing when this additional credit goes, not to entrepreneurs, but to Ponzi merchants in the finance sector, who use it not to innovate or add to productive capacity, but to gamble on asset prices. This adds to debt levels without adding to the economy's capacity to service them, leading to a blowout in the ratio of private debt to GDP. Ultimately, this process leads to a crisis like the one we are now in, where so much debt has been taken on that the growth of debt comes to an end. The economy then enters not a recession, but a Depression.

---

[36] Schumpeter, Joseph Alois. 1934. *The Theory of Economic Development : An Inquiry into Profits, Capital, Credit, Interest and the Business Cycle.* Cambridge, Massachusetts: Harvard University Press.

Developing an economics for the post-crisis world

For a while though, it looked like a recovery was afoot: growth did rebound from the depths of the Great Recession, and very quickly compared to the Great Depression (though slowly when compared to Post-WWII recessions).

Clearly the scale of government spending, and the enormous increase in Base Money by Bernanke, had some impact – but nowhere near as much as they were hoping for. However the main factor that caused the brief recovery – and will also cause the dreaded "double dip" – is the Credit Accelerator.

I've previously called this the "Credit Impulse" (sing the name bestowed by Michael Biggs et al., 2010)[37], but I think "Credit Accelerator" is both move evocative and more accurate. The Credit Accelerator at any point in time is the change in the change in debt over previous year, divided by the GDP figure for that point in time. From first principles, here is why it matters.

Firstly, and contrary to the neoclassical model, a capitalist economy is characterized by excess supply at virtually all times: there is normally excess labor and excess productive capacity, even during booms. This is not per se a bad thing but merely an inherent characteristic of capitalism – and it is one of the reasons that capitalist economies generate a much higher rate of innovation than did socialist economies[38] (Kornai 1980). The main constraint facing capitalist economies is therefore not supply, but demand.

Secondly, all demand is monetary, and there are two sources of money: incomes, *and the change in debt*. The second factor is ignored by neoclassical economics, but is vital to understanding a capitalist economy. Aggregate demand is therefore equal to Aggregate Supply *plus the change in debt*.

Thirdly, this Aggregate Demand is expended not merely on new goods and services, but also on net sales of existing assets. Walras' Law, that mainstay of neoclassical economics, is thus false in a credit-based economy – which

[37] Biggs, Michael; Thomas Mayer and Andreas Pick. 2010. "Credit and Economic Recovery: Demystifying Phoenix Miracles." *SSRN eLibrary*.
[38] Kornai, Janos. 1980. "'Hard' and 'Soft' Budget Constraint." *Acta Oeconomica*, 25(3-4), 231-45.

Economic growth, asset markets and the credit accelerator

happens to be the type of economy in which we live. Its replacement is the following expression, where the left hand is monetary demand and the right hand is the monetary value of production and asset sales:

Income + Change in Debt = Output + Net Asset Sales;

In symbols (where I'm using an arrow to indicate the direction of causation rather than an equals sign), this is:

$$Y + \frac{d}{dt}D \rightarrow GDP + NAS$$

This means that it is impossible to separate the study of "Finance" – largely, the behaviour of asset markets – from the study of macroeconomics. Income and new credit are expended on both newly produced goods and services, and the two are as entwined as a scrambled egg.

Net Asset Sales can be broken down into three components:
- The asset price Level; times
- The fraction of assets sold; times
- The quantity of assets

Putting this in symbols:

$$NAS = P_A \cdot \sigma_A \cdot Q_A$$

That covers the levels of aggregate demand, aggregate supply and net asset sales. To consider economic growth – and asset price change – we have to look at the rate of change. That leads to the expression:

$$\frac{d}{dt}Y + \frac{d^2}{dt^2}D \rightarrow \frac{d}{dt}GDP + \frac{d}{dt}NAS$$

Therefore the rate of change of asset prices is related to the **acceleration** of debt. It's not the only factor obviously – change in incomes is also a factor, and as Schumpeter argued, there will be a link between accelerating debt and rising income *if* that debt is used to finance entrepreneurial activity. Our great misfortune is that accelerating debt hasn't been primarily used for that purpose, but has instead financed asset price bubbles.

There isn't a one-to-one link between accelerating debt and asset price rises: some of the borrowed money drives up production (think SUVs during the boom), consumer prices, the fraction of existing assets sold, and the production of new assets (think McMansions during the boom). But the more the economy becomes a disguised Ponzi Scheme, the more the acceleration of debt turns up in rising asset prices.

As Schumpeter's analysis shows, accelerating debt should lead change in output in a well-functioning economy; we unfortunately live in a Ponzi economy where accelerating debt leads to asset price bubbles.

In a well-functioning economy, periods of acceleration of debt would be followed by periods of deceleration, so that the ratio of debt to GDP cycled but did not rise over time. In a Ponzi economy, the acceleration of debt remains positive most of the time, leading not merely to cycles in the debt to GDP ratio, but a secular trend towards rising debt. When that trend exhausts itself, a Depression ensues – which is where we are now. Deleveraging replaces rising debt, the debt to GDP ratio falls, and debt starts to reduce aggregate demand rather than increase it as happens during a boom.

Even in that situation, however, the acceleration of debt can still give the economy a temporary boost – as Biggs, Meyer and Pick pointed out. A slowdown in the rate of decline of debt means that debt is accelerating: therefore even when aggregate private debt is falling – as it has since 2009 – a slowdown in that rate of decline can give the economy a boost.

That's the major factor that generated the apparent recovery from the Great Recession: a slowdown in the rate of decline of private debt gave the economy a temporary boost. The same force caused the apparent boom of the Great Moderation: it wasn't "improved monetary policy" that caused the Great Moderation, as Bernanke once argued[39], but bad monetary policy that wrongly ignored the impact of rising private debt upon the economy.

---

[39] Bernanke, Ben S. 2004. "The Great Moderation: Remarks by Governor Ben S. Bernanke at the Meetings of the Eastern Economic Association, Washington, Dc

The factor that makes the recent recovery phase different to all previous ones – save the Great Depression itself – is that this strong boost from the Credit Accelerator has occurred while the *change in private debt* is still massively negative. I return to this point later when considering why the recovery is now petering out.

Figure 36

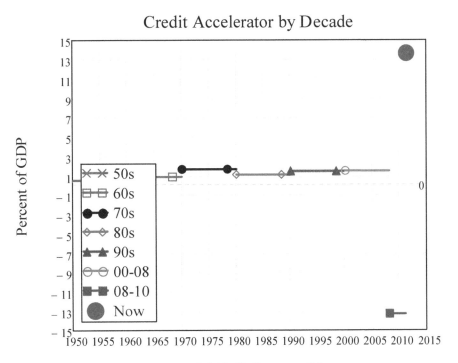

Credit Accelerator by Decade

www.debtdeflation.com/blogs

The last 20 years of economic data shows the impact that the Credit Accelerator has on the economy. The recent recovery in unemployment was largely caused by the dramatic reversal of the Credit Accelerator – from strongly negative to strongly positive – since late 2009:

February 20, 2004," *Eastern Economic Association.* Washington, DC: Federal Reserve Board.

Figure 37

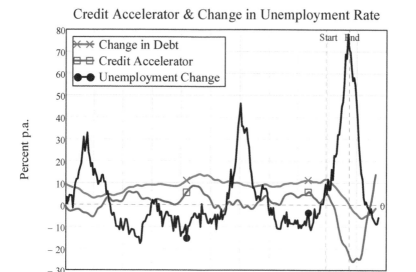

Credit Accelerator & Change in Unemployment Rate

www.debtdeflation.com/blogs

The Credit Accelerator also caused the temporary recovery in house prices:

Figure 38

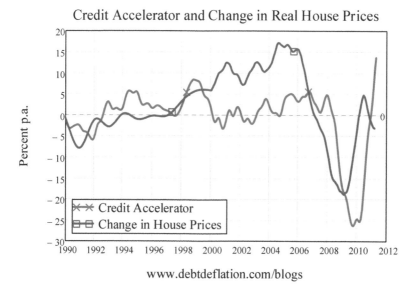

Credit Accelerator and Change in Real House Prices

www.debtdeflation.com/blogs

Economic growth, asset markets and the credit accelerator

And it was the primary factor driving the Bear Market rally in the stock market:

Figure 39

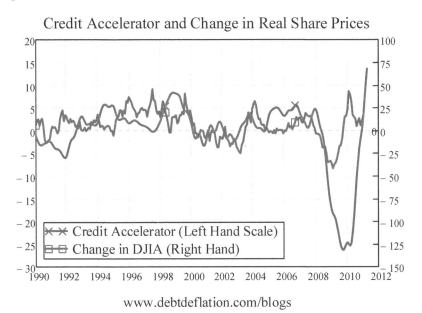

Credit Accelerator and Change in Real Share Prices

www.debtdeflation.com/blogs

Leads and lags

I use the change in the change in debt over a year because the monthly and quarterly data is simply too volatile; the annual change data smooths out much of the noise. Consequently the data shown for change in unemployment, house prices and the stock market are also for the change the previous year.

However the change in the change in debt operates can impact rapidly on some markets – notably the Stock Market. So though the correlations in the above graphs are already high, they are higher still when we consider the causal role of the debt accelerator in changing the level of aggregate demand by lagging the data.

This shows that the annual Credit Accelerator leads annual changes in unemployment by roughly 5 months, and its maximum correlation is a staggering -0.85 (negative because an acceleration in debt causes a fall in unemployment by boosting aggregate demand, while a deceleration in debt causes a rise in unemployment by reducing aggregate demand).

Figure 40

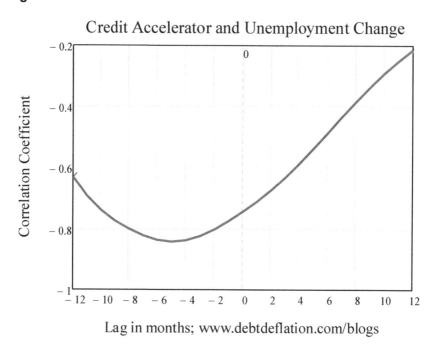

Credit Accelerator and Unemployment Change

Lag in months; www.debtdeflation.com/blogs

The correlation between the annual Credit Accelerator and annual change in real house prices peaks at about 0.7 roughly 9 months ahead:

Figure 41

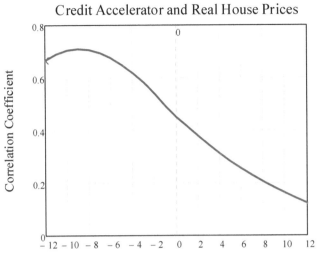

Credit Accelerator and Real House Prices

Lag in months; www.debtdeflation.com/blogs

And the Stock Market is also a creature of the Credit Impulse, where the lead is about 10 months and the correlation peaks at just under 0.6:

Figure 42

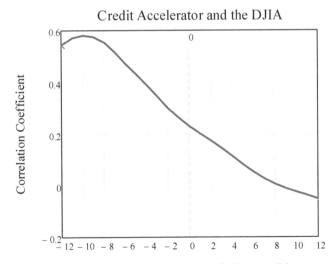

Credit Accelerator and the DJIA

Lag in months; www.debtdeflation.com/blogs

The causal relationship between the acceleration of debt and change in stock prices is more obvious when the 10 month lag is taken into account:

Figure 43

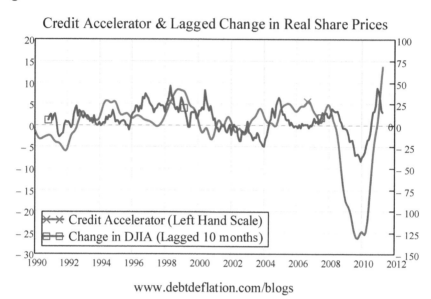

Credit Accelerator & Lagged Change in Real Share Prices

These correlations, which confirm the causal argument made between the acceleration of debt and the change in asset prices, expose the dangerous positive feedback loop in which the economy has been trapped. This is similar to what George Soros calls a reflexive process: we borrow money to gamble on rising asset prices, and the acceleration of debt causes asset prices to rise.

This is the basis of a Ponzi Scheme, and it is also why the Scheme must eventually fail. Because it relies not merely on growing debt, but accelerating debt, ultimately that acceleration must end – because otherwise debt would become infinite. When the acceleration of debt ceases, asset prices collapse.

The annual Credit Accelerator is still very strong right now – so why is unemployment rising and both housing and stocks falling? Here we have to look at the more recent quarterly changes in the Credit Accelerator – even though there is too much noise in the data to use it as a decent indicator (the quarterly levels show in Figure 44 are from month to month – so that the bar for March 2011 indicates the acceleration of debt between January and March 2011). It's apparent that the strong acceleration of debt in mid to late 2010 is petering out. Another quarter of that low a rate of acceleration in debt – or a return to more deceleration – will drive the annual Credit Accelerator down or even negative again. The lead between the annual Credit Accelerator and the annualized rates of change of unemployment and asset prices means that this diminished stimulus from accelerating debt is turning up in the data now.

Figure 44

Annual & Quarterly Credit Accelerator

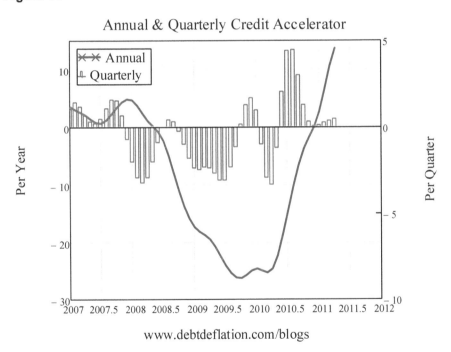

www.debtdeflation.com/blogs

This tendency for the Credit Accelerator to turn negative after a brief bout of being positive is likely to be with us for some time. In a well-functioning economy, the Credit Accelerator would fluctuate around slightly above zero. It would be above zero when a Schumpeterian boom was in progress, below during a slump, and tend to exceed zero slightly over time because positive credit growth is needed to sustain economic growth. This would result in a private debt to GDP level that fluctuated around a positive level, as output grew cyclically in proportion to the rising debt.

Instead, it has been kept positive over an unprecedented period by a Ponzi-oriented financial sector, which was allowed to get away with it by naïve neoclassical economists in positions of authority. The consequence was a secular tendency for the debt to GDP ratio to rise. This was the danger Minsky tried to raise awareness of in his Financial Instability Hypothesis (Minsky 1972) – which neoclassical economists like Bernanke ignored.

The false prosperity this accelerating debt caused led to the fantasy of "The Great Moderation" taking hold amongst neoclassical economists. Ultimately, in 2008, this fantasy came crashing down when the impossibility of maintaining a positive acceleration in debt forever hit – and the Great Recession began.

Figure 45

Level, Rate of change & Acceleration of Debt

www.debtdeflation.com/blogs

Economic growth, asset markets and the credit accelerator

From now on, unless we do the sensible thing of abolishing debt that should never have been created in the first place, we are likely to be subject to wild gyrations in the Credit Accelerator, and a general tendency for it to be negative rather than positive. With debt still at levels that dwarf previous speculative peaks, the positive feedback between accelerating debt and rising asset prices can only last for a short time, since it if were to persist, debt levels would ultimately have to rise once more. Instead, what is likely to happen is a period of strong acceleration in debt (caused by a slowdown in the rate of decline of debt) and rising asset prices – followed by a decline in the acceleration as the velocity of debt approaches zero.

Figure 46

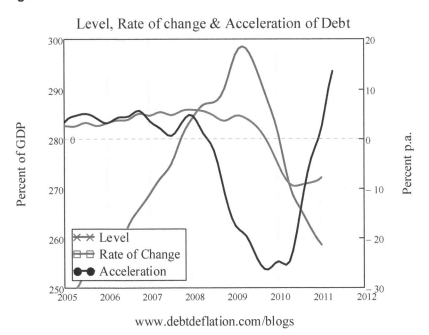

Level, Rate of change & Acceleration of Debt

www.debtdeflation.com/blogs

Here Soros's reflexivity starts to work in reverse. With the Credit Accelerator going into reverse, asset prices plunge – which further reduces the public's willingness to take on debt, which causes asset prices to fall even further.

105

The process eventually exhausts itself as the debt to GDP ratio falls. But given that the current private debt level is perhaps 170% of GDP above where it should be (the level that finances entrepreneurial investment rather than Ponzi Schemes), the end game here will be many years in the future. The only sure road to recovery is debt abolition – but that will require defeating the political power of the finance sector, and ending the influence of neoclassical economists on economic policy. That day is still a long way off.

Figure 47

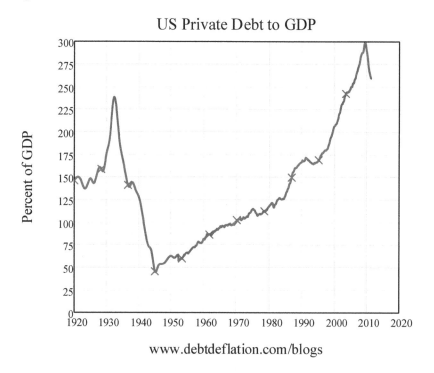

US Private Debt to GDP

www.debtdeflation.com/blogs

The return of the Bear

Far be it from me to underestimate the stock market's capacity to pluck the embers of delusion from the fire of reality. However, the crash in prices and explosion in volatility that began in late July 2011 may be evidence that sanity is finally making a comeback. What many hoped was a new Bull Market from the depths of the 52% crash from October 2007 till March 2009 was instead a classic Bear Market rally, fuelled by the market's capacity for self-delusion, accelerating private debt, and – thanks to QE2 – an ample supply of government-created liquidity. The 85% rise from March 2009 till April 2011 was enough to restore Wall Street's euphoria, but still fell short of the 110% rally needed to restore the 2007 peak.

That rally ended brutally in the last week of July. The S&P500 has fallen almost 250 points in less than a month, and is just a couple of per cent from a fully-fledged Bear Market.

Figure 48: Asset Prices versus Consumer Prices since 1890

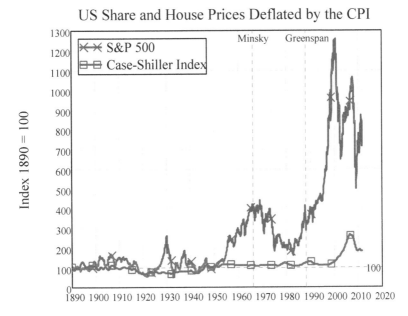

Figure 49: "Buy & Hold" anyone?

S&P500 Since 2000

www.debtdeflation.com/blogs

The belief that the financial crisis was behind us, that growth had resumed, and that a new bull market was warranted, have finally wilted in the face of the reality that growth is tepid at best, and likely to give way to the dreaded "Double Dip". The "Great Recession" – which Kenneth Rogoff correctly noted should really be called the "Second Great Contraction" – is therefore still with us, and will not end until private debt levels are dramatically lower than today's 260 per cent of GDP (see Figure 51).

Figure 50: Growth peters out

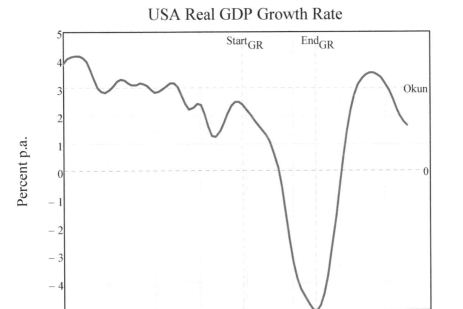

USA Real GDP Growth Rate

www.debtdeflation.com/blogs

With reality back in vogue, it's time to revisit some of the key insights of the one great economic realist of the last 50 years, Hyman Minsky. A good place to start is Figure 48 above, which shows the relationship between asset prices and consumer prices in America over the last 120 years.

One essential aspect of Minsky's Financial Instability Hypothesis was the argument that there are two price levels in capitalism: consumer prices, which are largely set by a markup on the costs of production, and asset prices, which are determined by expectations and leverage. This argument originated with Keynes in Chapter 17 of the General Theory, when he noted that investment is motivated by the desire to produce "those assets of which the normal supply-price is less than the demand price" (Keynes 1936, p. 228), and expressed more clearly in "The General Theory of Employment", where he argued that the scale of production of capital assets "depends, of course, on the relation between their costs of production and the prices which they are expected to realise in the market" (Keynes 1937, p. 217). Minsky significantly elaborated upon this point, and this – as much as his focus upon uncertainty – was a key point of divergence from the neoclassical interpretation of Keynes:

> "The perception that the quantity of money determines the price level of capital assets, for any given set of expecta-tions with respect to quasi-rents and state of uncertainty, because it affects the financing conditions for positions in capital assets, implies that in a capitalist economy there are two "price levels," one of current output and the second of capital assets. A fundamental insight of Keynes is that an economic theory that is relevant to a capitalist economy must explicitly deal with these two sets of prices. Economic theory must be based upon a perception that there are two sets of prices to be determined, and they are determined in different markets and react to quite different phenomena. Thus, the relation of these prices-say, the ratio-varies, and the variations affect system behavior. "When economic the-ory followed Sir John Hicks and phrased the liquidity preference function as a relation between the money supply and the interest rate, the deep significance of Keynesian theory as a theory of behavior of a capitalist economy was lost" (Minsky 1982, p. 79).

Over the very long term, these two price levels have to converge, because ultimately the debt that finances asset purchases must be serviced by the sale of goods and services – you can't forever delay the Day of Reckoning by borrowing more money. But in the short term, a wedge can be driven between them by rising leverage.

Unfortunately, in modern capitalism, the short term can last a very long time. In America's case, this short term lasted 50 years, as debt rose from 43 per cent of GDP in 1945 to over 300 per cent in early 2009. The finance sector always has a proclivity to fund Ponzi Schemes, but since World War II this has been aided and abetted by a government and central bank nexus that sees rising asset prices as a good thing.

The most egregious cheerleader for asset price inflation was Alan Greenspan. That's why I've marked Greenspan on Figure 48 and Figure 51: if his rescue of Wall Street after the 1987 Stock Market Crash hadn't occurred, it is quite possible that the unwinding of this speculative debt bubble could have begun twenty years earlier.

Figure 51: US Private Debt to GDP since 1920

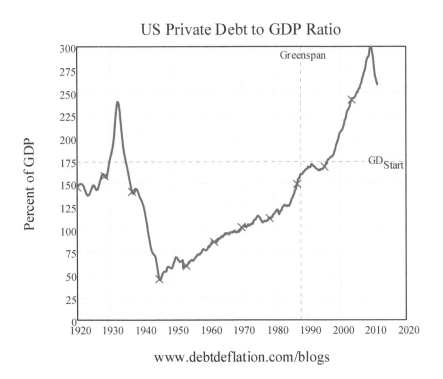

A mini-Depression would have resulted, as deleveraging drove aggregate demand below aggregate supply, but it would have been a much milder event than both the Great Depression and what we are experiencing now. The debt to GDP ratio in 1987 was slightly lower than at the start of the

Great Depression (159 versus 172 per cent), inflation was higher (4.5 per cent versus half a per cent), and the "automatic stabilizers" of government spending and taxation would have attenuated the severity of the drop in aggregate demand.

Instead, Greenspan's rescue – and the "Greenspan Put" that resulted from numerous other rescues – encouraged the greatest debt bubble in history to form. This in turn drove the greatest divergence between asset and consumer prices that we've ever seen.

The crisis began in late 2007 because rising asset prices require not merely rising debt, but accelerating debt. The great acceleration in debt that the Federal Reserve encouraged and the US financial system eagerly financed, ended in 2008 (see Figure 52).

Figure 52: Acceleration of Debt and the Bear Market Rally

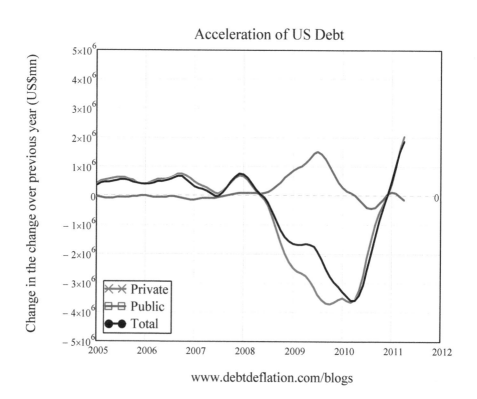

www.debtdeflation.com/blogs

From 1950 till 2008, the Credit Accelerator[40] averaged 1.1 per cent. In the depths of the downturn, it hit minus 26 per cent. With the motive force of accelerating debt removed, asset prices began their long overdue crash back to earth.

However the share market rebounded again because, partly under the influence of government and Central Bank policy, private debt accelerated once more even though, in the aggregate, *private debt was still falling*. The annual Credit Accelerator turned around from minus 26 per cent in 2010 to plus 3 per cent in early 2011.

Figure 53: Private debt accelerated even though the level was still falling

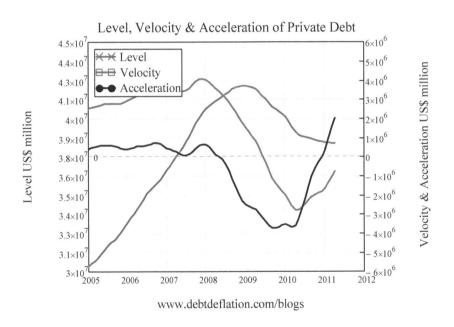

From 1950 till 2008, the Credit Accelerator[40] averaged 1.1 per cent.

---

[40] This is the ratio of the acceleration in private debt to GDP. The concept was originally called the Credit Impulse by Biggs, Meyer et al 2010 (Biggs, M., T. Mayer and A. Pick (2010). "Credit and Economic Recovery: Demystifying Phoenix Miracles." SSRN eLibrary.); I believe that Accelerator is a better term than Impulse. I am still refining the concept, and—as a dynamic modeller rather than a statistician—I may make some stumbles along the way. Nevertheless, the correlation between the Credit Accelerator and change in stock indices shown in Figure 7 is 0.26 over a 25 year period, and it is highly significant.

This in turn fed into the stock market, causing one of the biggest year-on-year rallies ever seen (see Figure 54). But it could not be sustained because, if debt continued to accelerate, then ultimately the level of debt relative to income would again start to rise. With all sectors of the US economy maxed out on credit (apart from the Government itself), this wasn't going to happen. The impetus from the Credit Accelerator thus ran out, and the Stock Market began its plunge back toward reality.

Figure 54: Accelerating debt drives rising share prices – and decelerating debt causes crashes

The Credit Accelerator & Change in Share Prices

www.debtdeflation.com/blogs

The stock market could easily bounce again from its current levels if, once again, the rate of decline of debt slows down. But in an environment where deleveraging dominates, deceleration will be the dominant trend in debt, and the unwinding of asset prices back towards consumer prices will continue.

How far could it go? Take another look at Figure 48. The CPI-deflated share market index averaged 113 from 1890 till 1950, with no trend at all: by 1950

114

it was back to the level of 1890. But from 1950 on, it rose till a peak of 438 in 1966 – which is the year that Hyman Minsky identified as the point at which the US passed from a financially robust to a financially fragile system. Writing in 1982, he observed that:

> "A close examination of experience since World War II shows that the era quite naturally falls into two parts. The first part, which ran for almost twenty years (1948-1966), was an era of largely tranquil progress. This was followed by an era of increasing turbulence, which has continued until today" (Minsky 1982, p. 6).[41]

From then, it slid back towards the long term norm, under the influence of the economic chaos of the late 60s to early 80s, only to take off in 1984 when debt began to accelerate markedly once more (see the inflexion point in 1984 in Figure 51). From its post-1966 low of 157 in mid-1982, the CPI-deflated S&P500 index rose to 471 in 1994 as the 1990s recession ended, and then took off towards the stratosphere during the Telecommunications and DotCom bubbles of the 1990s. Its peak of 1256 in mid-2000 was more than ten times the pre-1950 average.

Even after the falls of the past week, it is still at 709, while private debt, even after falling by 40% of GDP since 2009, is still 90 per cent of GDP above the level that precipitated the Great Depression – leaving plenty of energy in the debt-deleveraging process to take asset prices further down.

---

[41] Minsky elaborated that:
"Instead of an inflationary explosion at the war's end, there was a gradual and often tentative expansion of debt-financed spending by households and business firms. The newfound liquidity was gradually absorbed, and the regulations and standards that determined permissible contracts were gradually relaxed. Only as the successful performance of the economy attenuated the fear of another great depression did households, businesses, and financial institutions increase the ratios of debts to income and of debts to liquid assets so that these ratios rose to levels that had ruled prior to the Great Depression. *As the financial system became more heavily weighted with layered private debts, the susceptibility of the financial structure to disturbances increased. With these disturbances, the economy moved to the turbulent regime that still rules*" (pp. 7- 8; emphasis added).

There CPI-deflated share index doesn't have to return to the level of 1890-1950 – especially since companies like Berkshire-Hathaway that don't pay dividends give a legitimate reason for share prices to rise relative to consumer prices over time.[42] But a fall of at least 50 per cent is needed simply to bring the ratio back to its 1960s level.

Welcome to the Bear Market and the Second Great Contraction.

References:

Biggs, Michael; Thomas Mayer and Andreas Pick. 2010. "Credit and Economic Recovery: Demystifying Phoenix Miracles." SSRN eLibrary.

Keynes, J. M. 1937. "The General Theory of Employment," The Quarterly Journal Of Economics, 51(2), 209-23.

Keynes, J. M. 1936. The General Theory of Employment, Interest and Money. London: Macmillan.

Minsky, Hyman P. 1982. Can "It" Happen Again? : Essays on Instability and Finance. Armonk, N.Y.: M.E. Sharpe.

---

[42] However these firms are in the minority; they attenuate the degree of divergence between share and consumer prices, but they are a sideshow compared to the explosion in the ratio since 1982.

The fiscal cliff – lessons from the 1930s
Report to US Congress, 6 December 2012

The "fiscal cliff" developed because both sides of the House concurred that reducing the growth of government debt was the most important economic policy objective, but they could not agree on a common program to do so. Instead, a program of indiscriminate spending cuts and tax concession abolitions was passed, as a "Sword of Damocles" that would drop on America's collective head if Congress could not reach a compromise by the end of 2012. So unless a deal is bartered by December 31st a set of tax increases and across-the-board cuts in government expenditure will reduce net government spending by about \$500 billion, or roughly three per cent of GDP.

What will the consequences be? As Mark Twain once observed, "The art of prophecy is very difficult, especially about the future", but it's fair to say that both Democrats and Republicans now fear what this future might be. The fantasy that reducing the government deficit might actually stimulate the economy has clearly been abandoned, in the light of the tragic results of austerity programs in Europe. But both parties can see no other way to achieve their shared overarching objective of reducing government debt.

Pardon me for questioning bipartisanship in this fractious age, but it's quite possible that the one thing Democrats and Republicans can agree on – that reducing government debt is the number one economic objective – is a mistake. A close look at the empirical data from America's last great financial crisis – the Great Depression – implies that reducing government debt now may hurt the private sector far more than it helps it, and may also throw America back into recession.

My starting point is an empirically based approach to macroeconomics which concludes that aggregate demand in a monetary economy is the sum of income plus the change in debt. I won't go into the mathematics of this argument here; instead, I'll show how this perspective explains why both the Great Depression and our current economic crisis occurred. It also implies that the fiscal cliff could tip the USA back into recession, while doing precious little to reduce government debt as a percentage of GDP.

Firstly, let's look at the recession as most economists do, by considering just GDP. Figure 55 shows both nominal and inflation adjusted GDP[43]. Notice that nominal GDP continued to grow for about 6 months after the official start of the recession, while inflation adjusted (or "real") GDP flatlined for about six months before it started to fall. Notice also that while GDP certainly fell, it doesn't look like a lot of a drop – certainly not when compared to the Great Depression. So why was it described as "the biggest crisis since the Great Depression"?

Figure 55: GDP in current dollars and adjusted for inflation (2005 dollars)

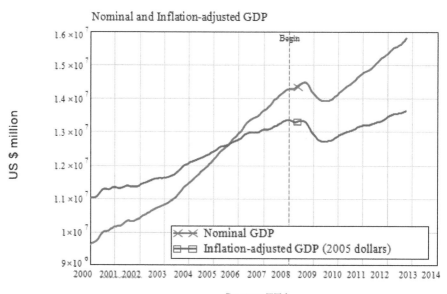

Source: BEA

---

[43] The marker "Begin" shows the start of the recession.

Figure 56: Aggregate US debt levels and GDP

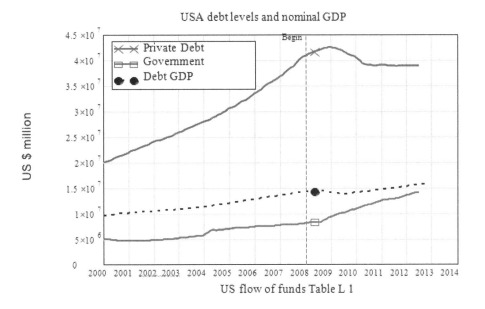

Here's where debt comes in. We all know that debt played a big role in the crisis, so, let's get some perspective on it – both private and public debt. Which do you think is bigger – private sector debt, or public sector debt? With all the hullabaloo about how public debt is imposing a burden on our children, you'd be forgiven for nominating public debt as the bigger of the two. You'd be wrong: even after the growth of public debt and deleveraging by the private sector in the last five years, public sector debt is still less than 40 per cent of the level of private debt, as Figure 56 shows.

Notice also that private debt rose at an accelerating rate from 2000 until it peaked in 2009, and then fell sharply, after which it flatlined from 2010 on. In contrast, government debt flatlined across 2000-2004, rose slowly in 2004-2008, and only took off in mid-2008 – at the same time as the decline in GDP began.

Figure 57: Annual change in debt and the level of GDP

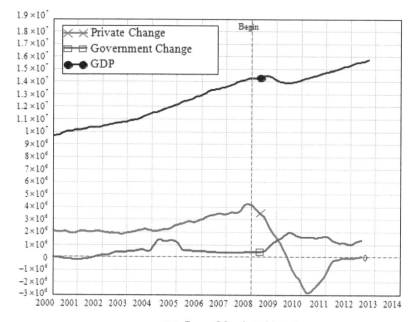

Annual change in debt and nominal GDP

US flow of funds Table L 1

Let's look at the same data from the point of view of GDP and the change in debt. Figure 57 shows GDP and the annual change in both private and government debt, and it highlights several important points.

- Firstly, the growth of private debt every year from 2000 to 2009 was higher than the highest growth of public debt. In 2008, private debt grew by over $4 trillion (when GDP was just over $14 trillion). Government debt rose by $2 trillion in 2009, which is a lot. But it was no more than the annual growth in private debt in every year from 2000 till 2009, and less than half the peak level of growth of private debt.

- Secondly, the recession began precisely when the rate of increase of private debt peaked and began to fall.
- Thirdly, the "fiscal crisis" – the sudden rapid increase in the government deficit – didn't start until six months after the economic crisis began, when nominal GDP also began to fall.

Already, these observations imply that the change in the behavior of private debt played a key role in the crisis, and that the increase in government spending was a reaction to the downturn in the real economy.

Figure 58 brings this data together in the context of my argument that the change in debt adds to aggregate demand. The black line in Figure 58 shows GDP alone; the red line shows GDP plus the change in private debt only; the blue line shows GDP plus the change in both private and government debt.

Now I think you can see both the timing and the severity of the crisis. The decline in private sector aggregate demand (the sum of GDP plus the change in private debt) was huge. It peaked at $18.4 trillion at the beginning of 2008 and then plunged to $11.1 trillion by early 2010 – a fall of 38 per cent that caused unemployment to explode and asset markets to collapse (see Figure 59 and Figure 60).

Figure 58: GDP plus change in debt from 2000 until today

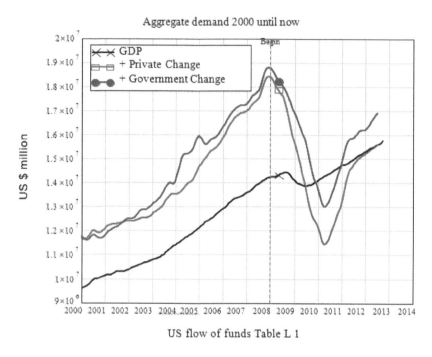

US flow of funds Table L 1

Figure 59: The causal link between change in debt and unemployment

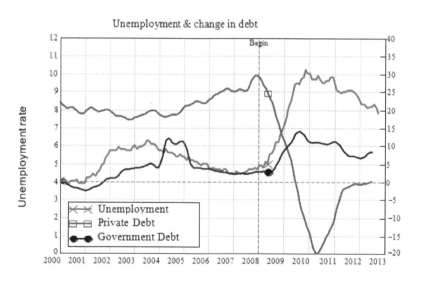

The change in government sector debt cushioned the blow of this dramatic private sector collapse. Total aggregate demand in 2008 (the sum of GDP plus the change in both private and government debt) peaked at $18.8 trillion, and fell to $13 trillion – a 31 per cent fall in total demand. This is still a huge fall – greater than anything experienced since the Great Depression – but it is substantially less than the fall in private sector demand alone.

Since the depths of the crisis in 2010, the private sector has largely stopped deleveraging: private debt is neither rising nor falling, so that the change in private sector debt is having no overall impact on aggregate demand. But public debt, which is still rising, is adding over $1 trillion to spending in the economy at present. Without the public sector deficit right now, total cash flow in the economy would be roughly $15.5 trillion; because of the public sector deficit, total spending is closer to $17 trillion.

Change in debt and employment

The impact of the collapse in the growth of private debt was immense: it caused both the explosion in unemployment and the collapse of asset markets. Figure 59 shows the correlation between change in debt and unemployment: the rise in unemployment in 2008 coincided with the turnaround from growing to shrinking private debt. Then the strengthening of the recovery in 2010 coincided with a slowdown in the rate of decline of private debt. The correlation between the change in private debt and the level of unemployment is -0.94: rising private debt causes falling unemployment.

That's not to say that rising private debt is a good thing – far from it. A certain level of debt-financed growth is good, when that debt helps corporations invest in new products and technologies. But the dependence the US economy developed upon debt-financed growth far exceeded this good level.

What about the relationship between change in government debt and unemployment? That's the opposite of the private sector debt to unemployment relation: while rising private debt is correlated with falling unemployment, rising government debt is associated with rising unemployment: the correlation coefficient is a positive 0.81.

How can we make sense of this? Here it's obvious that government debt is responding to changes in the real economy: a rising level of unemployment means rising welfare payments and falling tax revenue. So rising unemployment causes rising government debt. The causal link runs from the real economy to government spending – at least when we're talking about spending that the government has little control over.

Since this rising debt adds cash flow to the economy, it also helps preserve some private sector employment: people receiving unemployment benefits go shopping at Wal-Mart and keep some of those private sector workers in employment. Without that debt-financed government spending, private sector unemployment could have risen a lot more than it actually did – a point I'll make later in comparing our crisis to the Great Depression.

Change in debt and asset markets

Asset markets display what engineers would call a "positive feedback loop" between asset prices and the change in debt: rising debt causes rising asset prices, and rising asset prices encourage more people to borrow to speculate. Such processes always break down – which is why real engineers take great care to eliminate or control positive feedback processes in systems like cars, rockets and even bridges. Unfortunately, "financial engineers" delight in amplifying these destructive positive feedback loops in the financial system, by supporting deregulation and inventing derivatives.

Figure 60 shows the impact of rising and then falling mortgage debt on house prices. The growth in house prices from 2000 until 2006 was driven by rising mortgage debt, the collapse in prices was triggered by the collapse in mortgage debt, and the recent recovery in house prices coincides with a slowdown in the rate of deleveraging by the household sector. The correlation coefficient here is 0.81.

Figure 60: Change in mortgage debt and house prices

Of course, the government can also make discretionary changes in its own spending. It can boost spending as with the original response to the crisis in 2008, or it can cut spending as will happen if the fiscal cliff actually comes to pass, and as has been happening in Europe with austerity programs. The important question now, as we approach the fiscal cliff, is what impact will this have on the economy?

There is also the counter-factual issue of what would have happened to private sector aggregate demand if the government had not "stepped into the breach" with the massive increase in its deficit back in 2008. Clearly the private sector has stopped deleveraging now: would it have done so if the government had done nothing – either by keeping its deficit constant (as it was roughly doing until mid-2008), or by actively trying to run a surplus? We can get some inkling on both these issues by looking back at the Great Depression.

Aggregate demand during the Great Depression

The dynamics of private and public debt now and in the 1920s-1940s are qualitatively identical: a private debt bubble financed the "Roaring Twenties"; this gave way to private sector deleveraging in the 1930s; and public debt rose as the private sector delevered, thus reducing the impact of the private sector's deleveraging. However the quantitative differences are immense.

Firstly, the decline in real GDP back in the Great Depression was much larger than this time around (Figure 61). It fell 28 per cent from the peak in 1930 to the trough in 1932, versus the five per cent fall from 2008 till June 2009. So either our crisis was much milder than the Great Depression, or something happened this time round to reduce its impact.

Figure 61: Nominal and inflation-adjusted GDP during the Great Depression

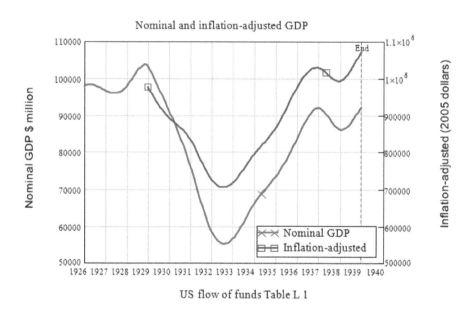

The second comparison lets us decide the "smaller crisis" versus "something happened" issue: even though the fall in GDP was much worse then, than now, the level of private was much lower in the 1920s (compare Figure 62

with Figure 56), and the fall in private sector aggregate demand was greater this time around. Compare Figure 63 with Figure 57: the more than $4 trillion increase in private debt in 2008 added 28 per cent to aggregate demand from GDP alone, while the $3 trillion reduction in private debt in 2010 deducted 21 per cent from it. The comparable figures were a ten per cent boost in 1927 and a 21 percent deduction in 1931.

Figure 62: Debt levels and Nominal GDP 1925-1939

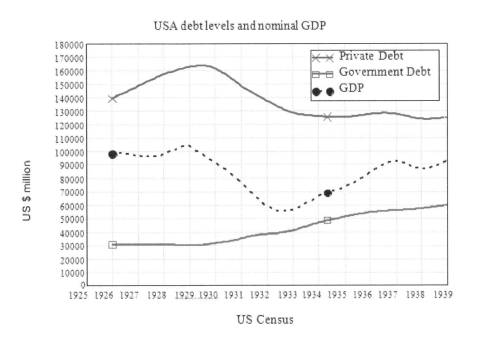

Figure 63: Nominal GDP and annual change in debt 1926-1939

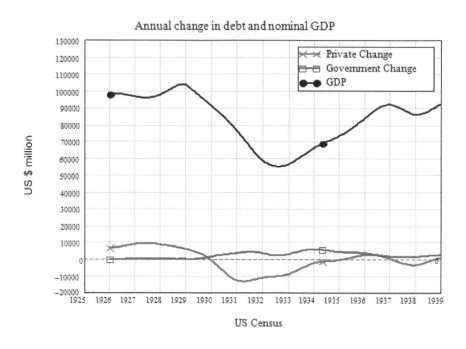

So aggregate demand fell from a greater height in our crisis, yet the impact on GDP was much less (compare Figure 64 with Figure 58). Something must have cushioned the blow. One candidate for that something else is the scale of government spending.

The increase in government spending in the Great Depression was slow in coming, and even the "New Deal", when it ultimately arrived, was relatively anemic compared to the stimulus in 2008-2010 (again, compare Figure 63 to Figure 57). Even though the "New Deal" is now a byword for government stimulus programs (and some magnificent public infrastructure was created during it), the monetary stimulus from government spending during the New Deal added nine per cent to private sector demand (the gap between the blue and red lines, divided by the red line). During our crisis, government spending added up to 15 per cent to private sector demand.

But it wasn't just the government spending itself that rescued the economy more rapidly today: it was the impact of that spending on the private sector's deleveraging. As Figure 63 shows, the private sector delevered for almost five years during the Great Depression – from 1930 until 1935. This time round private sector deleveraging lasted only two years – from mid-2009 till mid-2011 (check Figure 57). If that government spending hadn't risen as much as it did, then conceivably the private sector's deleveraging could have gone on for a lot longer – and this crisis could have been much worse than it was.

This brings us to the fiscal cliff – and its forerunner in 1937.

Figure 64: GDP plus change in debt from 1925 until 1939

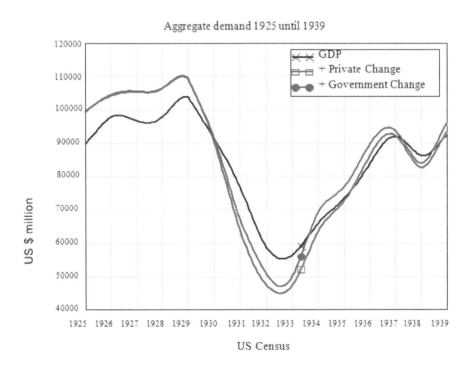

The fiscal cliff of 1937

As you can see from Figure 63 and Figure 65, the Roosevelt government "took its foot off the gas" from 1934 on as GDP started to recover. The government deficit peaked at $5.7 billion (yes, billion) in 1934 and fell to as little as $1.2 billion in 1937, in the belief that the worst was over and it was time to get the government's finances in order.

Only the worst wasn't over; it had merely been postponed because the private sector had stopped deleveraging in mid-1934 – probably in response to the extra demand being pumped into the economy via the New Deal. But it started to delever again in 1937, and kept doing it for another two years – probably in response to the drop in demand from the public sector. Unemployment, which had fallen from 25 per cent in 1933 to just over 10 per cent in 1937, exploded back to 20 per cent in 1938.

Figure 65: Unemployment and change in debt 1929-1939

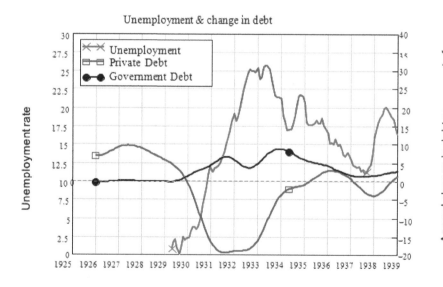

Escaping the Great Depression

Nominal GDP only began to recover strongly in 1940, when firstly private debt and then government debt began to rise far more rapidly – clearly as a consequence of the War in Europe (see Figure 66). Government debt finally exceeded GDP, and deficit-spending, and not austerity, led the USA out of the Great Depression. From 1936 until 1938 the government deficit virtually disappeared – and so too did the economic recovery. It only came back in earnest when the government threw fiscal caution to the wind, and geared up for the approaching conflict of WWII.

Figure 66: Aggregate US debt levels and GDP 1925-1945

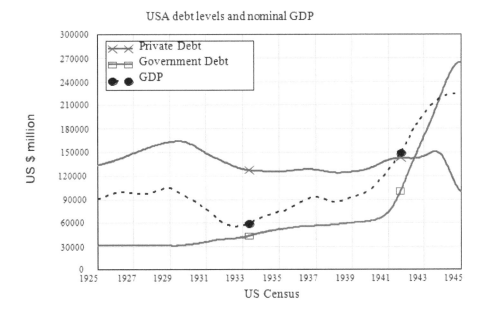

Figure 67: Annual change in debt and the level of GDP 1925-1945

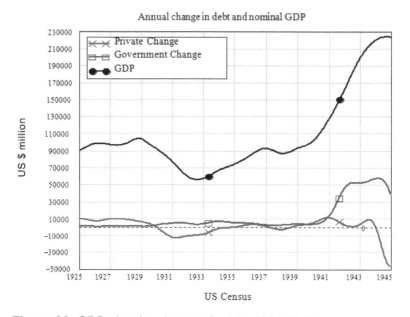

Figure 68: GDP plus the changes in debt 1925-1945

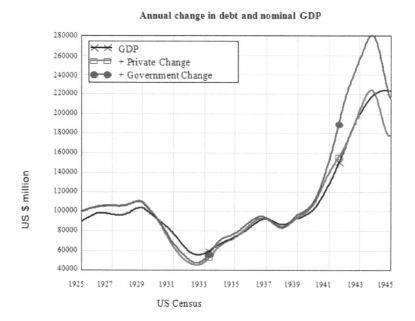

As the end of WWII approached, rising public debt was such a large contributor to aggregate demand that the private sector was able to reduce its debt dramatically – far more so than during the worst of the Great Depression – with only a small impact on GDP (see Figure 67). The public sector was able to easily reduce its debt levels in the booming economy of the early post-War years. (Unfortunately, over time the financial sector returned to the behavior that causes the Roaring Twenties bubble. Over the next 60 years, private sector debt rose from 45 per cent of GDP to 303 per cent in 2009. The comparable figure at the end of 1930 was 175 per cent of GDP.)

Figure 68 puts the whole story together in terms of the contributors to aggregate demand between the Roaring Twenties and the end of WWII (and compare this to Figure 58, to see how early we are in our own process of deleveraging from a level of private sector debt that should never have been allowed to accumulate in the first place).

This debt-focused analysis of the economy, and the history of the Great Depression, implies that the fiscal cliff could trigger a renewed period of private sector deleveraging that would put the economy back into a recession driven by falling private sector aggregate demand. There are therefore very good reasons to avoid the fiscal cliff, and to alter the public discourse on debt so that it focuses on the dominant problem, which is the private debt bubble that caused this crisis in the first place

Takeaway points

- Private debt and government debt are independent, but affect each other.
- Both boost demand in the economy when they rise, and reduce it when they fall.
- Private debt is more important than public debt because it is so much larger, and it drives the economy whereas government debt reacts to it.
- The crisis was caused by the growth of private debt collapsing.
- Government debt rose because the economy collapsed, and it reduced the severity of the crisis.

- A premature attempt to reduce government debt through "the fiscal cliff" could trigger a renewed bout of deleveraging by the private sector, which could push the economy back into a recession.
- For the foreseeable future, the main challenge of public policy will be not reducing government debt, but managing the impact of the much larger "Rock of Damocles" of private debt that hangs over the economy.

A bubble so big we can't even see it

What a difference three months makes. I first published this note on the topic of the stock market and whether it was in a bubble at the end of March ("The Debt Effect", *Business Spectator* 2013/03/30); at that stage the only apparent direction for the stock market was up. Now its volatility is starting, once again, to give traders nightmares.

Before the current turmoil began, Federal Reserve Chairman Ben Bernanke's hope was that rising asset prices would lead to a "wealth effect" that would encourage the American consumer to start spending again, and thus help the American economy finally leave the "Great Recession" behind. His predecessor Alan Greenspan argued in February that this would work because:

> "…the stock market is the really key player in the game of economic growth… The data shows that stock prices are not only a leading indicator of economic activity, they are a major cause of it. The statistics indicate that 6 percent of the change in GDP results from changes in market value of stocks and homes" (Greenspan 2013).

This is the so-called "wealth effect": an empirical relationship between change in the value of assets and the level of consumer spending which implies that an increase in wealth will cause an increase in consumption.

Greenspan's sage status is somewhat tarnished post-2007, so I don't think anyone should be surprised that his definitive statement involves a sleight of mouth. The "6 cents extra spending for every dollar increase in wealth" found in the research he alluded to was for the relationship between changes in the value of housing wealth and consumption, *not stocks*. In fact, the authors argued that the wealth effect from stocks was "statistically insignificant and economically small":

"Consistent and strong evidence is found for large but sluggish housing wealth effects... the MPC [marginal propensity to consume] out of a one dollar change in two-year lagged housing wealth is about 6 cents...

Furthermore, *a statistically insignificant and economically small stock wealth effect is found* ... Additionally, there is evidence that the housing wealth effect is significantly larger than the stock wealth effect... these results suggest that it is necessary to take into consideration the potentially substantial difference between consumers" respective reactions to fluctuations in the housing markets and stock markets" (Jorda, Schularick et al. 2011, p. 18. Emphasis added).

So the empirical data does not support Greenspan's notion that the stock market drives the economy (though the housing sector might). But equally the economy isn't booming sufficiently to make the reverse case that the economy drives the stock market. So what is causing the markets to boom right now?

Let's start by taking a closer look at the data than Alan did. There are a number of surprises when one does – even for me. Frankly, I did *not* expect to see some of the results I show here: as I used to frequently tell my students before the financial crisis began, I wouldn't dare make up the numbers I found in the actual data. That theme continues with margin debt for the USA, which I've only just located (I expected it to be in the Federal Reserve Flow of Funds, and it wasn't – instead it's recorded by the New York Stock Exchange).

The first surprise came when comparing the S&P500 to the Consumer Price Index over the last century – since what really tells you whether the stock market is "performing well" is not just whether it's rising, but whether it's rising faster than consumer prices. Figure 69 shows the S&P500 and the US CPI from the same common date – 1890 – until today.

A bubble so big we can't even see it

In contrast to house prices, there are good reasons to expect stock prices to rise faster than consumer prices (two of which are the reinvestment of retained earnings, and the existence of firms like Microsoft and Berkshire Hathaway that don't pay dividends at all). I therefore expected to see a sustained divergence over time, with of course periods of booms and crashes in stock prices.

Figure 69: The S&PP500 and the CPI from 1890 till today

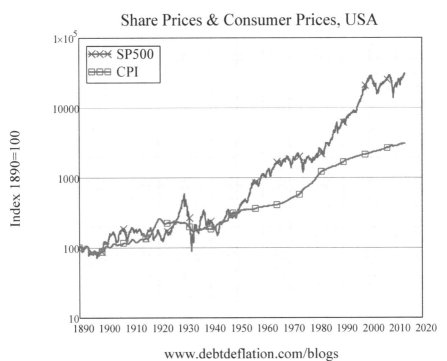

That wasn't what the data revealed at all. Instead, there was a period from 1890 till 1950 where there was no sustained divergence, while almost all of the growth of share prices relative to consumer prices appeared to have occurred since 1980. Figure 70 illustrates this by showing the ratio of the S&P500 to the CPI – starting from 1890 when the ratio is set to 1. The result shocked me – even though I'm a dyed in the wool cynic about the stock market. The divergence between stock prices and consumer prices, which virtually everyone (me included) has come to regard as the normal state of affairs, began in earnest only in 1982. Until then, apart from a couple of little bubbles in stock prices in 1929 (yes I'm being somewhat ironic, but take a look at the chart!) and 1966, there had been precious little real divergence between stock prices and consumer prices.

Figure 70: Ratio of stock prices to consumer prices from 1890 till todays

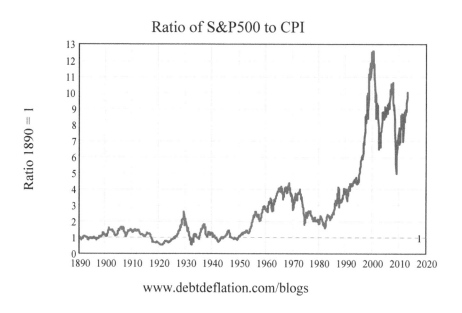

Ratio of S&P500 to CPI

www.debtdeflation.com/blogs

And then, boom! What must certainly be the biggest bubble in stock prices in human history took off – and it went hyper-exponential in 1995.

In 1982, the ratio of stock prices to consumer prices was only 1.8 times what it was in 1915. By 1990, the ratio was substantial at 4 times – well above the level of 1929 (2.6:1) but below the peak reached back in 1966 (4.1:1). Then it just exploded to 12.5 times by the peak of the DotCom bubble in 2000.

Since then, it's been doing the Jitterbug. The current rally has erased the crash of 2008 in nominal terms, but at a ratio of just over 10:1 today, it still stands shy of the two previous peaks of 12.5:1 in 2000 and 10.5 in 2008.

A bubble so big we can't even see it

So are stocks in a bubble? On this view, yes – and they have been in it since 1982. It has grown so big that – without a long term perspective – it isn't even visible to us. It has almost burst on two occasions – in 2000 and 2008 – but even these declines, as precipitous as they felt at the time, reached apogees that exceeded the previous perigees in1929 and 1968.

But this of itself doesn't truly establish that there is a bubble however, since as noted, even I expected to see a trend in the ratio of stock prices to consumer prices over time. Perhaps 1890-1950 was the abnormal and this is now a restoration of it?

So is there any other series that looks anything like this? Oh, let's try one at random – say, the ratio of margin debt (on the New York Stock Exchange) to GDP (see Figure 71).

Figure 71: NYSE Margin debt as percentage of GDP

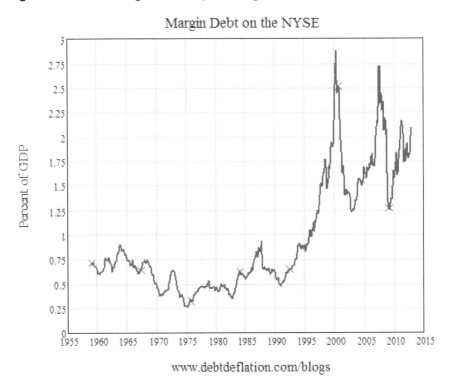

OK, I had my tongue in my cheek, but again this data had even me gob smacked when I first plotted it. I had *not* expected this correlation: my analysis actually runs from change in margin debt, rather than its level. So this outright match blew me away – particularly when I put the two series on the same chart (see Figure 72 – and yes Alan, feel free to use this one on the ABC News!).

Figure 72: Margin debt compared to the DJIA – correlation 0.945

My causal argument commences from my definition of aggregate demand as being the sum of GDP plus the change in debt – a concept that at present only heretics like myself, Michael Hudson, Dirk Bezemer and Richard Werner assert, but which I hope will become mainstream one day. Matched to this is a redefinition of supply to include not only goods and services but also turnover on asset markets.

This implies a causal link between the rate of change of debt and the level of asset prices, and therefore between the acceleration of debt and the rate of change of asset prices – but not one between the level of debt and the level of asset prices. Nonetheless there is one in the US data, and it's a doozy: the correlation between the level of margin debt and the level of the Dow Jones is 0.945.

Of course there are elements of spurious correlation here: they were both generally rising over 1955-2013. But one can also make a causal argument that increasing levels of debt levered up the gap between asset and consumer prices. This assertion of course directly contradicts a famous proposition in academic finance – the "Modigliani-Miller theorem" that the level of debt has no impact on the level of asset prices – which is another good reason to take it seriously.

In devising my "aggregate demand is income plus change in debt; aggregate supply is goods and services plus net turnover on asset markets" relation, I was never sure whether the measure of asset market turnover should be based on the level of asset prices, or their rate of change: this was something that only empirical research could clarify. And on this point, the US data is again exceptional: both the rate of change of margin debt (relative to GDP) and the rate of acceleration of margin debt correlate strongly with change in the Dow over the past six decades.

The correlation of the change in debt with change in the Dow is stronger than the correlation of acceleration – 0.59 versus 0.4 – but both are pretty strong for correlations over more than half a century, especially since conventional wisdom asserts they should both be zero.

Figure 73: Change in margin debt & change in the Dow – correlation 0.59

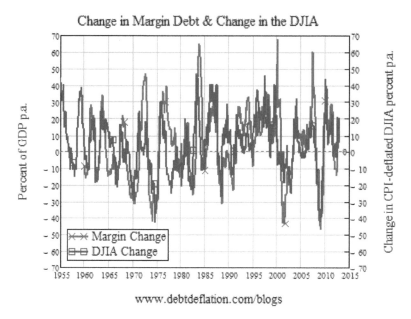

Figure 74: Margin debt acceleration & change in the Dow – correlation 0.4

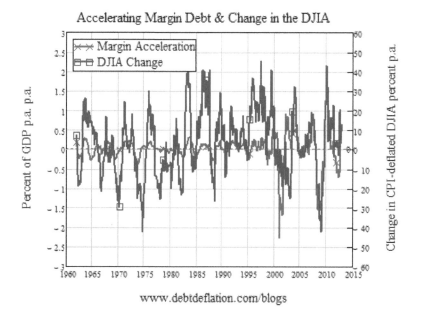

The correlations have risen too as the level of debt has risen – both aggregate private debt and, in the USA's case, margin debt which is specifically used to buy shares.

Figure 75: Change in margin debt & the Dow in recent years – correlation 0.69

Change in Margin Debt & Change in the DJIA

www.debtdeflation.com/blogs

143

Figure 76: Margin debt acceleration & change in the Dow – correlation 0.6

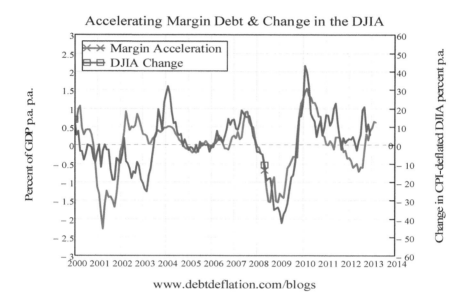

Accelerating Margin Debt & Change in the DJIA

www.debtdeflation.com/blogs

Now comes the complex question: which causes which? Does rising/accelerating margin debt cause the stock market to rise, or does a rising stock market entice more people into margin debt? Obviously there will be some cumulative causation here: both statements are going to be true to some degree. But this also implies a positive feedback loop, which is part of the explanation for why stock prices are so volatile.

Regardless of that complex causal loop, this data scotches Greenspan and his causal argument that a rising stock market causes a rising GDP. The market – and recently the economy – has risen not because of "the wealth effect", but because of "the leverage effect". Leverage has returned to the stock market, driving up stock prices and aggregate demand in the process.

How far can it go? Margin debt is still shy of its all-time high as a percentage of GDP, so there is certainly some headroom for further rises. But at the same time, the market is still in territory that was uncharted before the Loony Zeros (my "Roaring Twenties" candidate for how we should describe the last decade and a half) drove it higher than it has ever been before. Fragility, rather than sustainability is the message I would take from this data.

I'm reassured in this prognosis by the fact that Greenspan made precisely the opposite point in that interview, when he stated that "the price-earnings ratio is at a level at which it cannot basically go down very much." As some other commentators have observed, Greenspan expressing confidence in the stock market is a reliable contrary indicator.

References

Bernanke, B. (2002). Deflation: Making Sure "It" Doesn't Happen Here. Washington, Federal Reserve Board.

Biggs, M. and T. Mayer (2010). "The Output Gap Conundrum." *Intereconomics/Review of European Economic Policy* 45(1): 11-16.

Biggs, M., T. Mayer and A. Pick (2010). "Credit and Economic Recovery: Demystifying Phoenix Miracles." SSRN eLibrary.

Eggertsson, G. B. and P. Krugman (2012). "Debt, Deleveraging, and the Liquidity Trap: A Fisher-Minsky-Koo approach." *Quarterly Journal of Economics* 127: 1469–1513.

Fiebiger, B. (2014). "Bank credit, financial intermediation and the distribution of national income all matter to macroeconomics." *Review of Keynesian Economics* 2(3): 292-311.

Greenspan, A. (2013). "Greenspan: Ignore The Economy, 'Only The Stock Market Matters'".*Zerohedge* http://www.zerohedge.com/news/2013-02-15/greenspan-ignore-economy-only-stock-market-matters.

Jorda, O., M. H. P. Schularick and A. M. Taylor (2011). "Financial Crises, Credit Booms, and External Imbalances: 140 Years of Lessons." *IMF Economic Review* 59(2): 340-378.

Keen, S. (1995). "Finance and Economic Breakdown: Modeling Minsky's 'Financial Instability Hypothesis'." *Journal of Post Keynesian Economics* 17(4): 607-635.

Keen, S. (2014). "Endogenous money and effective demand." *Review of Keynesian Economics* 2(3): 271 – 291.

Keen, S. (2015). "The Macroeconomics of Endogenous Money: Response to Fiebiger, Palley & Lavoie." *Review of Keynesian Economics* forthcoming 3(2).

Keen, S. (2015). "Post Keynesian Theories of Crisis." *American Journal of Economics and Sociology* forthcoming.

Keynes, J. M. (1936). *The general theory of employment, interest and money*. London, Macmillan.

Keynes, J. M. (1937). "The General Theory of Employment." *The Quarterly Journal of Economics* 51(2): 209-223.

Kornai, J. (1980). "'Hard' and 'Soft' Budget Constraint." *Acta Oeconomica* 25(3-4): 231-245.

Krugman, P. (2012). *End this Depression Now!* New York, W.W. Norton.

Krugman, P. (2012). "Minsky and Methodology (Wonkish)." *The Conscience of a Liberal*   http://krugman.blogs.nytimes.com/2012/03/27/minksy-and-methodology-wonkish/.

Krugman, P. (2013). "Secular Stagnation Arithmetic." *The Conscience of a Liberal* http://krugman.blogs.nytimes.com/2013/12/07/secular-stagnation-arithmetic/.

Krugman, P. (2013). "Secular Stagnation, Coalmines, Bubbles, and Larry Summers." *The Conscience of a Liberal* http://krugman.blogs.nytimes.com/2013/11/16/secular-stagnation-coalmines-bubbles-and-larry-summers/?_r=0.

Lavoie, M. (2014). "A comment on 'Endogenous money and effective demand': a revolution or a step backwards?" *Review of Keynesian Economics* 2(3): 321 - 332.

Lebergott, S. (1954). "Measuring Unemployment." *The Review of Economics and Statistics* 36(4): 390-400.

Lebergott, S. (1986). "Discussion of Romer and Weir Papers." *The Journal of Economic History* 46(2): 367-371.

Lucas, R. E., Jr. (2003). "Macroeconomic Priorities." *American Economic Review* 93(1): 1-14.

Minsky, H. P. (1972). Financial instability revisited: the economics of disaster. Reappraisal of the Federal Reserve Discount Mechanism. B. o. G. o. t. F. R. System. Washington, D.C., Board of Governors of the Federal Reserve System: pp. 95-136.

Minsky, H. P. (1982). *Can "it" happen again? : essays on instability and finance.* Armonk, N.Y., M.E. Sharpe.

Moore, B. J. (1979). "The Endogenous Money Stock." *Journal of Post Keynesian Economics* 2(1): 49-70.

Prescott, E. C. (1999). "Some Observations on the Great Depression." *Federal Reserve Bank of Minneapolis Quarterly Review* 23(1): 25-31.

Romer, C. (1986). "Spurious Volatility in Historical Unemployment Data." *Journal of Political Economy* 94(1): 1-37.

Rowe, N. (2013). "What Steve Keen is maybe trying to say." *Worthwhile Canadian Initiative*   http://worthwhile.typepad.com/worthwhile_canadian_initi/2013/08/what-steve-keen-is-maybe-trying-to-say.html.

Secular stagnation and endogenous money

The crisis of 2007/08 has generated many anomalies for conventional economic theory, not the least that it happened in the first place. Though mainstream economic thought has many channels, the common belief before this crisis was that either crises cannot occur (Prescott 1999), or that the odds of such events had either been reduced (Bernanke 2002) or eliminated (Lucas 2003) courtesy of the scientific understanding of the economy that mainstream theory had developed.

This anomaly remains unresolved, but time has added another that is more pressing: the fact that the downturn has persisted for so long after the crisis. Recently Larry Summers suggested a feasible explanation in a speech at the IMF. "Secular stagnation", Summers suggested, was the real explanation for the continuing slump, and it had been with us for long before this crisis began. Its visibility was obscured by the Subprime Bubble, but once that burst, it was evident.

This hypothesis asserts, in effect, that the crisis itself was a second-order event: the main event was a tendency to inadequate private sector demand which may have existed for decades, and has only been masked by a sequence of bubbles. The policy implication of this hypothesis is that generating adequate demand to ensure full employment in the future may require a permanent stimulus from the government – meaning both the Congress and the Fed – and perhaps the regular creation of asset market bubbles.

What could be causing the secular stagnation – if it exists? Krugman (Krugman 2013) noted a couple of factors: a slowdown in population growth (which is obviously happening: see Figure 77); and "a Bob Gordonesque decline in innovation" (which is rather more conjectural).

Though Summers' thesis has its mainstream critics, there's a chorus of New Keynesian support for the "secular stagnation" argument, which implies it will soon become the conventional explanation for the persistence of this slump long after the initial financial crisis has passed.

Krugman's change of tune here is representative. His most recent book-length foray into what caused the crisis – and what policy would get us out of it – was entitled *End This Depression NOW!* The title, as well as the book's contents, proclaimed that this crisis could be ended "in the blink of an eye". All it would take, Krugman then proposed, was a sufficiently large fiscal stimulus to help us escape the "Zero Lower Bound":

> "The sources of our suffering are relatively trivial in the scheme of things, and could be fixed quickly and fairly easily if enough people in positions of power understood the realities…"

One main theme of this book has been that in a deeply depressed economy, in which the interest rates that the monetary authorities can control are near zero, we need more, not less, government spending. A burst of federal spending is what ended the Great Depression, and we desperately need something similar today (Paul Krugman, 2012, pp. 23, 231).

Figure 77: Population growth rates are slowing

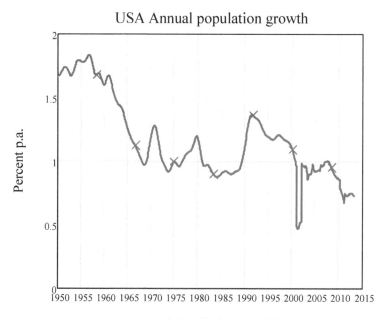

www.debtdeflation.com/blogs

Secular stagnation and endogenous money

Post-Summers, Krugman is suggesting that a short, sharp burst of government spending will **not** be enough to restore "the old normal". Instead, to achieve pre-crisis rates of growth in future – and pre-crisis levels of unemployment – permanent government deficits, and permanent Federal Reserve spiking of the asset market punch via QE and the like, may be required.

Not only that, but past apparent growth successes – such as "The Period Previously Known as The Great Moderation" – may simply have been above-stagnation rates of growth motivated by bubbles:

> "So how can you reconcile repeated bubbles with an economy showing no sign of inflationary pressures? Summers's answer is that we may be an economy that needs bubbles just to achieve something near full employment – that in the absence of bubbles the economy has a negative natural rate of interest. And this hasn't just been true since the 2008 financial crisis; it has arguably been true, although perhaps with increasing severity, since the 1980s" (Krugman 2013).

This argument elevates the "Zero Lower Bound" from being merely an explanation for the Great Recession to a General Theory of Macroeconomics: if the ZLB is a permanent state of affairs given secular stagnation, then permanent government stimulus and permanent bubbles may be needed to overcome it:

> "One way to get there would be to reconstruct our whole monetary system – say, eliminate paper money and pay negative interest rates on deposits. Another way would be to take advantage of the next boom – whether it's a bubble or driven by expansionary fiscal policy – to push inflation substantially higher, and keep it there. Or maybe, possibly, we could go the Krugman 1998/Abe 2013 route of pushing up inflation through the sheer power of self-fulfilling expectations" (Krugman 2013).

So is secular stagnation *the* answer to the puzzle of why the economy hasn't recovered post the crisis? And is permanently blowing bubbles (as well as permanent fiscal deficits) the solution?

Firstly there is ample evidence for a slowdown in the rate of economic growth over time – as well as its precipitate fall during and after the crisis.

Figure 78: A secular slowdown in growth caused by a secular trend to stagnation

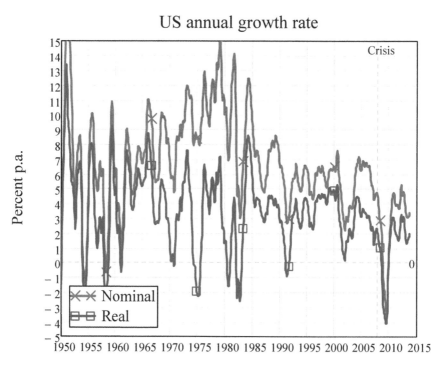

www.debtdeflation.com/blogs

The growth rate was as high as 4.4% p.a. on average from 1950-1970, but fell to about 3.2% p.a. from 1970-2000 and was only 2.7% in the Naughties prior to the crisis – after which it has plunged to an average of just 0.9% p.a. (see Table 8).

Table 8: US Real growth rates per annum by decade

Start	End	Growth rate p.y. for decade	Growth rate since 1950
1950	1960	4.2	4.2
1960	1970	4.6	4.4
1970	1980	3.2	4
1980	1990	3.1	3.8
1990	2000	3.2	3.7
2000	2008	2.7	3.5
2008	Now	0.9	3.3

So the sustained growth rate of the US economy *is* lower now than it was in the 1950s – 1970s, and the undoubted demographic trend that Krugman nominates is clearly one factor in this decline.

Another factor that Krugman alludes to in his post is the rise in household debt during 1980-2010 – which at first glance is incompatible with the "Loanable Funds" model of lending to which he subscribes.[44] In the Loanable Funds model, the aggregate level of debt (and changes in that level) are irrelevant to macroeconomics – only the distribution of debt can have significance:

> "Ignoring the foreign component, or looking at the world as a whole, we see that the overall level of debt makes no difference to aggregate net worth – one person's liability is another person's asset. It follows that the level of debt matters only if the distribution of net worth matters, if highly indebted players face different constraints from players with low debt" (Krugman 2012, p. 146).

---

[44] I won't consider other potential causes here. These range from the rather more dubious suggestion of a decline in innovation made by Krugman, to factors that Neoclassical economists like Krugman dismiss but others have proposed as major factors – such as the relocation of production from the USA to low wage countries – to factors on which there is more agreement, such as the rise in inequality.

Furthermore, the distribution of debt can only have macroeconomic significance at peculiar times, when the market mechanism is unable to function because the "natural rate of interest" – the real interest rate that will clear the market for Loanable Funds, and lead to zero inflation with other markets (including labor) in equilibrium – is negative.

Prior to Summers's thesis, Krugman had argued that this peculiar period began in 2008 when the economy entered a "Liquidity Trap". Private debt matters during a Liquidity Trap because lenders, worried about the capacity of borrowers to repay, impose a limit on debt that forces borrowers to repay their debt and spend less. To maintain the full-employment equilibrium, people who were once lenders have to spend more to compensate for the fall in spending by now debt-constrained borrowers.

But lenders are patient people, who by definition have a lower rate of time preference than borrowers, who are impatient people:

> "Now, if people are borrowing, other people must be lending. What induced the necessary lending? Higher real interest rates, which encouraged "patient" economic agents to spend less than their incomes while the impatient spent more" (Krugman, 2012, "Deleveraging and the Depression Gang").

The problem in a Liquidity Trap is that rates can't go low enough to encourage patient agents to spend enough to compensate for the decline in spending by now debt-constrained impatient agents.

> "You might think that the process would be symmetric: debtors pay down their debt, while creditors are correspondingly induced to spend more by low real interest rates. And it would be symmetric if the shock were small enough. In fact, however, the deleveraging shock has been so large that we're hard up against the zero lower bound; interest rates can't go low enough. And so we have a persistent excess of desired saving over desired investment, which is to say persistently inadequate demand, which is to

say a depression" (Krugman, 2012, "Deleveraging and the Depression Gang").

After Summers, Krugman started to surmise that the economy may have been experiencing secular stagnation since 1985, and that only the rise in household debt masked this phenomenon. Consequently the level and rate of change of private debt could have been macroeconomically significant not merely since 2008, but since as long ago as 1985.

Figure 79: Ratio of household debt to GDP

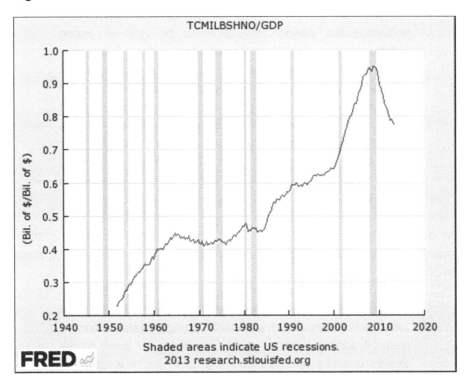

Commenting on the data (Figure 79, sourced from the St Louis Fed's excellent FRED database, is taken from Krugman's post), Krugman noted that perhaps the increase in debt from 1985 on masked the tendency to secular stagnation. Crucially, he proposed that the "natural rate of interest" was negative perhaps since 1985, and only the demand from borrowers kept

153

actual rates positive. This in turn implied that, absent bubbles in the stock and housing markets, the economy would have been in a liquidity trap since 1985:

> "There was a sharp increase in the ratio after World War II, but from a low base, as families moved to the suburbs and all that. Then there were about 25 years of rough stability, from 1960 to around 1985. After that, however, household debt rose rapidly and inexorably, until the crisis struck.
>
> So with all that household borrowing, you might have expected the period 1985-2007 to be one of strong inflationary pressure, high interest rates, or both. In fact, you see neither – this was the era of the Great Moderation, a time of low inflation and generally low interest rates. Without all that increase in household debt, interest rates would presumably have to have been considerably lower – maybe negative. In other words, you can argue that our economy has been trying to get into the liquidity trap for a number of years, and that it only avoided the trap for a while thanks to successive bubbles."

In general, the Loanable Funds model denies that private debt matters macroeconomically, as Krugman put it emphatically in a series of blog posts in 2012:

> "Keen then goes on to assert that lending is, by definition (at least as I understand it), an addition to aggregate demand. I guess I don't get that at all. *If I decide to cut back on my spending and stash the funds in a bank, which lends them out to someone else, this doesn't have to represent a net increase in demand.* Yes, in some (many) cases lending is associated with higher demand, because resources are being transferred to people with a higher propensity to spend; but Keen seems to be saying something else, and I'm not sure what. I think it has something to do with the notion that creating money = creating demand, but again

154

that isn't right in any model I understand" (Krugman 2012, emphasis added).

However, the Summers' conjecture provides a means by which private debt could assume macroeconomic significance since 1985 within the Loanable Funds model. Once secular stagnation commenced – driven, in this conjecture, by the actual drop in the rate of growth of population and a hypothesized decline in innovation – the economy was effectively in a liquidity trap, and somehow rising debt hid it from view.

That is the broad brush, but I expect that explaining this while remaining true to the Loanable Funds model will not be an easy task – since, like a Liquidity Trap itself, the Loanable Funds model is not symmetric. Whereas Krugman was able to explain how private debt causes aggregate demand to fall when debt is falling and remain true to the Loanable Funds model (in which banks are mere intermediaries and both banks and money can be ignored – see Eggertsson and Krugman 2012), it will be much harder to explain how debt adds to aggregate demand when it is rising. This case is easily made in an Endogenous Money model in which banks create new spending power, but it fundamentally clashes with Loanable Funds in which lending simply redistributes existing spending power from lenders to borrowers. Nonetheless, Krugman has made such a statement in a post-Summers blog:

> "Debt was rising by around 2 percent of GDP annually; that's not going to happen in future, which a naïve calculation suggests means a reduction in demand, other things equal, of around 2 percent of GDP" (Krugman 2013).

If he manages to produce such a model, and if it still maintains the Loanable Funds framework, then the model will need to show that private debt affects aggregate demand only during a period of either secular stagnation or a liquidity slump – otherwise the secular-stagnation-augmented Loanable Funds model will be a capitulation in all but name to the Endogenous Money camp (Rowe 2013).[45] Assuming that this is what Krugman will attempt, I

---

[45] Nick Rowe has shown how my oft-repeated shorthand that aggregate demand is income plus the change in debt can be expressed in a Neoclassical manner, so long as one acknowledges the Endogenous Money case that bank lending creates new

want to consider the empirical evidence on the relevance of private debt to macroeconomics. If it is indeed true that private debt only mattered post-1985, then this is compatible with a secular-stagnation-augmented Loanable Funds model – whatever that may turn out to be. But if private debt matters before 1985, when secular stagnation was clearly not an issue, then this points in the direction of Endogenous Money being the empirically correct model.

I will consider two indicators: the correlation between change in aggregate private nonfinancial sector debt and unemployment, and the correlation between the acceleration of aggregate private nonfinancial sector debt[46] and the change in unemployment. I am also using two much longer time series for debt and unemployment. Figure 80 extends Krugman's FRED chart by including business sector debt as well – and a longer term estimate for US debt that extends back to 1834. The unemployment data shown in Figure 81 is compiled from BLS and NBER statistics and Lebergott's estimates (Lebergott 1954, Lebergott 1986, Romer 1986) and extends back to 1890.

---

money: "Aggregate actual nominal income equals aggregate expected nominal income plus amount of new money created by the banking system minus increase in the stock of money demanded." However as well as abandoning Loanable Funds, this perspective requires abandoning equilibrium analysis as well: "We are talking about a Hayekian process in which individuals' plans and expectations are mutually inconsistent in aggregate. We are talking about a disequilibrium process in which people's plans and expectations get revised in the light of the surprises that occur because of that mutual inconsistency." I see both these as positive developments, but the habitual methods of Neoclassical economics may mean that these developments will not last.

[46] Defined as the change in the change in debt over a year (to crudely smooth the extremely volatile monthly data) divided by nominal GDP at the midpoint of the year.

Secular stagnation and endogenous money

Figure 80: Long term series on American private debt

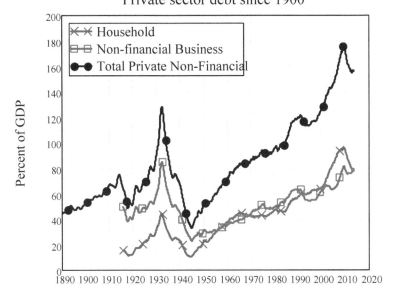

Private sector debt since 1900

www.debtdeflation.com/blogs

Figure 81: Correlation of change in aggregate private debt with unemployment

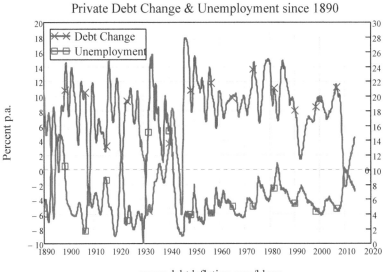

Private Debt Change & Unemployment since 1890

www.debtdeflation.com/blogs

157

Correlation is not causation as the cliché goes, but a correlation coefficient of -0.57 over almost 125 years implies that the change in debt has macroeconomic significance at all times – and not just during either secular stagnation or liquidity traps.

Table 9: Correlation of change in aggregate private debt with unemployment by decade

Start	End	Correlation with level of unemployment	
		Percentage change	Change as percent of GDP
1890	2013	-0.57	-0.51
1890	1930	-0.59	-0.6
1930	1940	-0.36	-0.38
1940	1950	0.15	0.32
1950	1960	-0.48	-0.28
1960	1970	-0.33	-0.58
1970	1980	-0.41	-0.37
1980	1990	-0.27	-0.55
1990	2000	-0.95	-0.95
2000	2013	-0.97	-0.95

Shorter time spans emphasize the point that neither secular stagnation nor liquidity traps can be invoked to explain why changes in the level of private debt have macroeconomic significance. Secular stagnation surely didn't apply between 1890 and 1930, yet the correlation is -0.6; neither secular stagnation nor a liquidity trap applied in the period from 1950 till 1970, yet the correlation is substantial in those years as well.

The correlation clearly jumps dramatically in the period after the Stock Market Crash of 1987, but that is more comfortably consistent with the basic Endogenous Money case that I have been making – that new private debt created by the banking sector adds to aggregate demand – than it will be with any secular-stagnation-augmented Loanable Funds model.

Secular stagnation and endogenous money

The debt acceleration data (Biggs and Mayer 2010, Biggs, Mayer et al. 2010) hammers this point even further. Figure 82 shows the acceleration of aggregate private sector debt and change in unemployment from 1955 (three years after quarterly data on debt first became available) till now. The correlation between the two series is -0.69.

Figure 82: Correlation of acceleration in aggregate private debt with change in unemployment

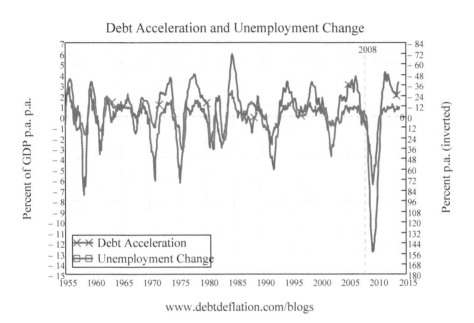

Debt Acceleration and Unemployment Change

www.debtdeflation.com/blogs

As with the change in debt and unemployment correlation, shorter time spans underline the message that private debt matters at all times. Though the correlation is strikingly higher since 1987 – a date I emphasize because I believe that Greenspan's actions in rescuing that bubble then led to the Ponzi economy that America has since become – it is high throughout, including in times when neither "secular stagnation" nor a "liquidity trap" can be invoked.

Table 10: Correlation of acceleration in aggregate private debt with change in unemployment by decade

Start	End	Correlation
1950	2013	-0.6
1950	1960	-0.53
1960	1970	-0.61
1970	1980	-0.79
1980	1990	-0.6
1990	2000	-0.86
2000	2013	-0.89

I await the IS-LM or New Keynesian DSGE model that Krugman will presumably produce to provide an explanation for the persistence of the crisis in terms that, however tortured, emanate from conventional economic logic in which banks and money are ignored (though private debt is finally considered), and in which everything happens in equilibrium. But however clever it might be, it will not be consistent with the data.

References

Bernanke, Ben. 2002. "Deflation: Making Sure 'It' Doesn't Happen Here," Washington: Federal Reserve Board.

Biggs, Michael and Thomas Mayer. 2010. "The Output Gap Conundrum." *Intereconomics/Review of European Economic Policy*, 45(1), 11-16.

Biggs, Michael; Thomas Mayer and Andreas Pick. 2010. "Credit and Economic Recovery: Demystifying Phoenix Miracles." *SSRN eLibrary*.

Eggertsson, Gauti B. and Paul Krugman. 2012. "Debt, Deleveraging, and the Liquidity Trap: A Fisher-Minsky-Koo Approach." *Quarterly Journal of Economics*, 127, 1469 – 513.

Krugman, Paul. 2012a. *End This Depression Now!* New York: W.W. Norton.

Krugman, Paul. 2012b. "Minsky and Methodology (Wonkish)," *The Conscience of a Liberal*. New York: New York Times.

Krugman, Paul. 2013a. "Secular Stagnation Arithmetic," P. Krugman, *The Conscience of a Liberal.* New York: New York Times.

Krugman, Paul. 2013b. "Secular Stagnation, Coalmines, Bubbles, and Larry Summers," P. Krugman, *The Conscience of a Liberal.* New York: New York Times.

Lebergott, Stanley. 1986. "Discussion of Romer and Weir Papers." *The Journal of Economic History*, 46(2), 367-71.

Lebergott, Stanley. 1954. "Measuring Unemployment." *The Review of Economics and Statistics*, 36(4), 390-400.

Lucas, Robert E., Jr. 2003. "Macroeconomic Priorities." *American Economic Review*, 93(1), 1-14.

Prescott, Edward C. 1999. "Some Observations on the Great Depression." *Federal Reserve Bank of Minneapolis Quarterly Review*, 23(1), 25-31.

Romer, Christina. 1986. "Spurious Volatility in Historical Unemployment Data." *Journal of Political Economy*, 94(1), 1-37.

Rowe, Nick. 2013. "What Steve Keen Is Maybe Trying to Say," N. Rowe, *Worthwhile Canadian Initiative.* Canada: Nick Rowe.

Lightning Source UK Ltd.
Milton Keynes UK
UKOW06f2025210316

270573UK00003B/23/P